D0875437

THE JACOBEAN POETS

The

Jacobean Poets

By EDMUND GOSSE

HON. M.A. TRINITY COLLEGE, CAMBRIDGE

GREENWOOD PRESS, PUBLISHERS
NEW YORK

Originally published in 1894
by Charles Scribner's Sons

First Greenwood Reprinting 1969

SBN 8371-2755-6

PRINTED IN UNITED STATES OF AMERICA

PREFACE.

IN this volume, for the first time, an attempt has been made to concentrate attention on what was produced in English poetry during the reign of James I., that is to say, during twenty-two years of the opening of the seventeenth century.

It is hoped that a certain freshness may be gained by approaching the subject from this empirical point of view, rather than, as hitherto has been the custom, by including the poets of James, and even of Charles, under the vague and conventional heading of " Elizabethan." It would not be wise, doubtless, to make a general habit of regarding literary history through artificial barriers of this kind; but for once, and in dealing with a fragment of such a hackneyed period, it is hoped that it may be found beneficial. The unparalleled wealth of English poetry during the reign of James I. will certainly strike the student, and in many cases he may be surprised to find that " Elizabethans " of the hand books had not emerged from childhood, or published a single copy of verses, when Elizabeth resigned the seat of kings to her cousin of Scotland.

This little volume, then, is an attempt to direct critical attention to all that was notable in English poetry from 1603 to 1625. The scope of the work has made it possible to introduce the names of many writers who are now for the first time chronicled in a work of this nature. The author believes the copious use of dates to be indispensable to the rapid and intelligent comprehension of literary history, and he has forced himself to supply as many as possible; the student will, however, not need to be reminded that in the dramatic chapters these must in large measure be regarded as conjectural. When we consider the vagueness of knowledge regarding the detail of Jacobean drama even a generation ago, it is surprising that scholarship has attained such a measure of exactitude, yet the discovery of a bundle of papers might at any moment disturb the ingenious constructions of our theoretical historians.

In selecting illustrative passages for quotation, the aim has been to find unfamiliar beauties rather than to reprint for the thousandth time what is familiar in every anthology.

E. G.

CONTENTS.

—◆◇◆—

CHAPTER   PAGE

      PREFACE   V

I.   THE LAST ELIZABETHANS   1

II.   BEN JONSON—CHAPMAN   23

III.   JOHN DONNE   47

IV.   BEAUMONT AND FLETCHER   68

V.   CAMPION — DRAYTON — DRUMMOND — SIR JOHN

      BEAUMONT   89

VI.   HEYWOOD—MIDDLETON—ROWLEY   116

VII.   GILES AND PHINEAS FLETCHER—BROWNE   ...   137

VIII.   TOURNEUR—WEBSTER—DAY—DABORNE   ...   159

IX.   WITHER—QUARLES—LORD BROOKE   181

X.   PHILIP MASSINGER   202

      INDEX   219

THE JACOBEAN POETS,

CHAPTER I.

THE LAST ELIZABETHANS.

Queen Elizabeth died on the 24th of March, 1603, and was conducted to the grave by the poets with innumerable "mournful ditties to a pleasant new tune," as one of the frankest of the rhymsters admitted. There were "elegies" and "lamentations," *"luctus"* and *"threnodia,"* at the disappearance from so large a scene of so dread a sovereign; and then, with the customary promptitude, there succeeded "panegyricks," and "congratulations," and "welcomes," and "wedding garments" addressed by humble eager versifiers to "serenissimum et potentissium Jacobum beatissimæ Elizabethæ legitime et auspicatissime succedentem." Before we consider what poetry was to be throughout the reign of the Scottish monarch so radiantly conducted to the throne of England, we may glance at what poetry had ceased to be by the time his predecessor died.

There is a danger which, of course, must be faced
and admitted, in our recognizing a hard-and-fast line of
demarcation between one epoch and another. Elizabethan faded silently into Jacobean, and no curtain
descended in 1603 which divided the earlier age from
the later. But we may with safety assert that certain
general features marked English poetry under the one
monarch, and did not mark it under the other. To
compare selected passages is notoriously unjust; but
without special unfairness it may be advanced that such a
stanza as the following is characteristically Elizabethan—

> Hark! hark! with what a pretty throat
> Poor robin-redbreast tunes his note;
> Hark! how the jolly cuckoos sing,
> Cuckoo! to welcome in the spring;

and this no less characteristically Jacobean—

> Who ever smelt the breath of morning flowers,
> New-sweeten'd with the dash of twilight showers,
> Of pounded amber, or the flowering thyme,
> Or purple violets in their proudest prime,
> Or swelling clusters from the cypress-tree?
> So sweet's my love, aye, far more sweet is he,
> So fair, so sweet, that heaven's bright eye is dim,
> And flowers have no scent, compar'd with him.

Of the two writers from whom quotation is here made,
the later possessed the stronger genius, but in straight-
forwardness and simplicity the former has the advantage.
What were lost were the clear morning note, the serenity,
the coolness, and sober sweetness of poets who had no
rivals in the immediate past. What were gained were
passion, depth of thought, a certain literary cleverness
(which was in itself a snare), and a closer pertinence to

passing events. Bohemia lost its seaports, the realms
of the Fairy Queen disappeared, when James I. came to
the throne. His subjects knew more than their fathers
had done, spoke out more boldly, were more boisterous
and demonstrative. Romance ceased to rule their day,
and in its place a certain realism came to the front. In
poetry, that tended to become turbid which had been so
transparent, and that conscious and artificial which had
been so natural and unaffected. Erudition became more
and more a feature of poetry, and the appeal to primitive
observations and emotions less piquant than references
to the extraordinary, the violent, and even the unwhole-
some. In this way, even in work of the magnificent first
decade of James I., we can see the sprouting of those
seeds which were to make a wilderness of poetry thirty
or forty years later. It will be desirable to examine as
closely as we can the aspects of the two schools of verse
at the arbitrary moment which we have chosen for the
opening date of this inquiry.

The mere knife-cut of a political event across the
texture of literature is not often of much use to those
who study literary history. But, as a matter of fact, the
year 1603 forms a more convenient point at which to
pass into a new condition of things than almost any
other neighbouring year would form. It is impossible,
of course, to pretend that a distinct line can be drawn
between Elizabethan and Jacobean poetry; but it is a
fact that while certain influences had by that year almost
ceased to act, other influences began, about that same
year, to make themselves felt. Before entering upon the
discussion of purely Jacobean verse, that is to say, of

the verse produced during the reign of James I., it will
be well to glance at what had been characteristic of
Elizabeth's reign, and had ceased to exist before the time
of her death.

In the first place, the primitive poetry which had
flourished at the beginning of her reign was all wasted
and gone. It had scarcely left behind it a trace of its
transitory charm. It had given way to firmer and more
brilliant kinds of writing. Three of its proficients lived
on, in extreme old age, into the reign of James. Of
these one was the venerable Bishop of Bath and Wells,
John Still (1543–1607), who, more than half a century
earlier, had opened the dance of English drama, with his
"right pithy, pleasant, and merry comedy entitled,
Gammer Gurton's Needle." Another was William Warner
(1558–1609), whose extremely popular *Albion's England,*
a rambling historical poem, first published nearly twenty
years earlier, was still in good repute among the lower
classes, and frequently reprinted. The third was "old
hoarse Palamon" of Spenser's *Colin Clout,* Thomas
Churchyard (1520?–1604), now at the very extremity of
his enormous life, but still pouring forth his doggerel
publications, three of which celebrated events of the new
reign. But all this primitive verse was utterly out of
fashion among educated people.

The first clear running of the pure pastoral sweetness
had also ceased. The deaths of Sidney and of Spenser,
before the sixteenth century had ended, had brought this
beautiful and genuinely Elizabethan poetry to a close.
In all of that body of verse, the imitation of ancient
work, conducted through a bright romantic medium, by

men who had before them the task of moulding the
language, as well as enlivening the imaginations of their
readers, had led to the creation of something very lucent,
fresh and delicate.   The light of daybreak was over this
unsullied and almost boyish pastoral poetry.   It was,
above all, chivalrous and impassioned, full of the pride
and glory of the times, a little artificial, a little strained
and unnatural, but crude and brilliant with the unchecked
fire and colour of adolescence.   With the removal of its
two great pioneers, this school of poetry was bound to
decline.   But the accidents which led to its entire disappearance before James ascended the throne are curious.
The dramatists whose lyrics are of this class will presently
be referred to.   But Lyly must be mentioned here as
the most pastoral, the most affectedly limpid of them all;
he was still alive, but completely silent, and soon, in
1606, to die.   Sir Edward Dyer (1550?–1607) was in
the same plight, and so was the "Ambrosiac Muse" of
Henry Constable (1562–1613).   In Watson had long
ago passed away a talent still more trivial, ingenious, and
innocent.   All those writers were wholly unlike the
coarser, opaquer and profounder Jacobeans.   The only
link between these men and the latter Spenserians, of
whom we shall have much to say in a subsequent
chapter, was the morbid and Italianized Richard Barnfield (1574–1627), who, though he outlived James, wrote
no verse after the death of Elizabeth.

Less easy to define, as an element closed up within
the reign of Elizabeth, was the first plaintive fervour of
religious poetry, Catholic or high-church.   The reign of
Elizabeth had not been, as that of her successor was

ultimately to be, rich in fine, devotional verse. But it had produced the martyr Robert Southwell (1562–1595), whose vivid and emotional canzonets and hymns had introduced a new element into English literature, an element not to be taken up again until nearly twenty years after his death at Tyburn, but from that time onward to be carried on and up till it culminated in the raptures of Crashaw.

The first outburst of simple lyrical writing, too, had come to an end. After the reign of Elizabeth, there was no longer a bird singing lustily and sweetly in every pamphlet or broadside bush. Francis Davison's *Poetical Rhapsody*, 1602, was the latest of those successive anthologies which for nearly half a century, from the publication of *Tottel's Miscellany* in 1557, had formed so prominent and so charming a feature in English poetical literature. This series of anthologies had culminated in *England's Helicon*, 1600, one of the richest and most inspired collections of miscellaneous verse ever published in any country, or at any time. In this divine volume the peculiar lyric of the Elizabethan age had found its apotheosis, and after this it very rapidly declined. Master Slender showed himself characteristically a man of his time, when he said, "I had rather than forty shillings I had my book of songs and sonnets here." The subject of James I., although he bought abundant reprints of these Elizabethan song-books, produced none that were new for himself, except as accompanied by, or written to music. The decline of universal lyrical gift is marked in the Jacobean period, and the songs which we come across in this volume will mainly be found to have been the work of belated Elizabethans.

Still more complete was the disappearance of the earliest school of Elizabethan drama, the coherent and serried body of playwrights, now generally known as the Precursors of Shakespeare. These men formed a school, the limits of which are clearly defined. Their leader and master was that noble genius, Christopher Marlowe; the other names best known to us are those of Greene, Peele, Kyd, and Nash. The biographies of these men are in most cases vague, but it seems certain that all four of them died, prematurely, during the last decade of Elizabeth's reign. Their solitary survivor, Lodge, lived on until the year of James I.'s death, but published no new verse or drama during the sixteenth century. Lyly, the Euphuist, too, was an active dramatist of a still more primitive class, who survived, but in entire silence. The first play-harvest was completely garnered before the new reign began, so completely that Shakespeare, and perhaps Dekker, are the only really transitional figures which are more Elizabethan than Jacobean.

Another class of production which had left its mark strongly on our literary development, and had stopped, or at least slackened, by 1603, was that of the great poetical translators. Early in Elizabeth's reign there had been a flock of semi-barbarous translators of the classics. If any one of these was still alive, it must have been Thomas Twyne, who continued the *Æneids* of Phaer. Later in the life of the same monarch, a far more literary and accomplished set of men enriched our language with versions of the Italian poets, Sir John Harington (1561–1612), aided by his brother Francis, translating Ariosto in 1591, and Tasso being carefully interpreted by Richard Carew (1555-1620) in 1594, and brilliantly by Edward Fairfax (1570?-1635) in 1600. Homer, first attempted in 1581 by Arthur Hall, had been nobly conquered by Chapman in 1598, and this last-named poet continued, as we shall see, through the reign of James, to annex first provinces of Greek poetry. But he was, by age and in spirit, an Elizabethan, and no true Jacobean was a great translator. Even Sir Arthur Gorges' *Lucan*, though not published until 1614, was in all probability written twenty years earlier.

One or two very early precursors of the Jacobeans were still alive in 1603. Sackville, Lord Buckhurst, whose gloomy and magnificent *Induction* is far more Jacobean in style than any of those compositions of Spenser's which succeeded it, was made Earl of Dorset by James I., and survived until 1608. His most famous poem, repeatedly re-issued after his death, continued to exercise an influence on the younger writers. Sir Walter Raleigh was not executed till 1618, but his later work as a versifier is largely conjectural. Sir John Davies, whose philosophical poems were among the most original and beautiful literary productions of the close of Elizabeth's reign, was suddenly silenced by the admiration James I. conceived for his judgment in practical affairs, and was henceforth wholly absorbed in politics. But an examination of Davies' work, had we space for it here, would form no ill preparation for the study of several classes of Jacobean poetry. He was eminently a writer before his time. His extremely ingenious *Orchestra*, a poem on dancing, has much in it that suggests the Fletchers on one

side and Donne on the other, while his more celebrated
magnum opus of the *Nosce Teipsum* is the general precursor of all the school of metaphysical ingenuity and
argumentative imagination.   In Davies there is hardly
a trace of those qualities which we have sought to distinguish as specially Elizabethan, and we have difficulty
in obliging ourselves to remember that his poems were
given to the public during the course of the sixteenth
century.   To the exquisite novelty and sweetness of his
Hymns of Astræa, critical justice has never yet been
done.   But we have no excuse for lingering any longer on
the works of a poet so exclusively of the reign of Elizabeth.   Barnaby Barnes (1559–1609), too, that isolated
Ronsardist among our London poets, published no lyrics
after 1595.   His plays, perhaps, were Jacobean, but
we possess only one of them, *The Devil's Charter*, not
printed till 1607, which seems to belong to the school
of Marlowe.   Joseph Hall, the satirist of the *Virgide-
miarum*, becoming Bishop of Exeter, wrote no more
verse, and died at length in 1656, by far the last survivor
of the Elizabethan choir.

Of all the writers of the age it is the laureate, Samuel
Daniel, whom it is most difficult to assign to either reign.
His literary activity is accurately balanced between the
two, and it seems impossible to decide whether he was
rather Elizabethan or Jacobean.   It may therefore be
convenient to come first to a consideration of his poems,
to which, however, from his historical position, the
prominence they discover must not here be awarded.
He was born near Taunton, in Somerset, in or about
1562, was educated at Magdalen College, Oxford,

resided at Wilton, and began to publish verses—the
Delia sonnets—in 1592. He went to Italy, where he met
Guarini and other leading men of letters, and deepened
the academic and literary tincture of his taste. On his
return to England, volume after volume, published in
quick succession, and collected as the *Poetical Essays
of Sam. Daniel* in 1595, testified to the fertility of his
fancy. These were lyrical, gnomic, and dramatic, sonnets,
odes, historical epics, and tragedies.

When the new king and queen were descending on
their capital, Daniel met them in Rutlandshire with a
Panegyric, which, although it was curiously blunt and
unflattering, secured him their cordial favour. He was
made licenser of plays, salaried master of the revels to her
Majesty, and unofficial laureate to the court of James I.,
where he was to the end a peculiarly favoured personage.
He retired at length to his native Somerset, and rented a
farm near Beckington, trying, if Fuller is to be believed,
to practise farming by the rules of Virgil's *Georgics*.
He died at the close of 1619, and was buried in
Beckington Church.

When the *Panegyrick at Burleigh Harrington* was
published in 1603, there were included with it not
merely a prose *Defence of Ryme*, which is of high interest and merit, and has remained, more or less, the code
of English prosody, but also a series of *Certain Epistles*
in verse. The *Panegyric*, which extends over more than
seventy stanzas of *ottava rima*, is a stately and didactic
piece of reflection on the moral conditions of the
moment, very interesting in its way, especially to an
historian, but somewhat prosaic.

The pulse of England never more did beat
  So strong as now ; nor ever were our hearts
Let out to hopes so spacious and so great
  As now they are ; nor ever in all parts
Did we thus feel so comfortable heat
  As now the glory of thy worth imparts ;
The whole complexion of the commonwealth,
So weak before, hoped never for more health.

Couldst thou but see from Dover to the Mount,
  From Totnes to the Orcades, what joy,
What cheer, what triumphs, and what dear account
  Is held of thy renown this blessed day !—
A day which we and ours must ever count
  Our solemn festival, as well we may ;
And though men thus count kings still which are new,
Yet do they more, where they find more is due.

The *Epistles*, on the other hand—with the exception
of his Elizabethan *Musophilus* (1599)—form Daniel's
most attractive contribution to poetry. It is his fault to
persist when he has ceased to be exhilarating, and these
Epistles—they are six in number—are all short. They
are essays on set moral themes addressed to persons of
nobility, in curiously novel and elaborate measures, and
their sustained flow of reflection, without imagery, without
ornament, is singularly dignified. The *Epistle to the
Countess of Cumberland* is probably the best-known of
Daniel's poems; that to the *Countess of Bedford*, in
terza rima, is perhaps even more gracefully conducted
to an academic close—

How oft are we forced on a cloudy heart
  To set a shining face, and make it clear,
Seeming content to put ourselves apart,

To bear a part of others' weaknesses !
  As if we only were composed by Art,
  Not Nature, and did all our deeds address
To opinion, not to a conscience, what is right,
  As framed by example, not advisedness,
  Into those forms that entertain our sight ;
And though books, Madam, cannot make this mind,
  Which we must bring apt to be set aright,
  Yet do they rectify it in that kind,
And touch it so, as that it turns that way
  Where judgment lies ; and though we cannot find
  The certain place of truth, yet do they stay
And entertain us near about the same ;
  And gives the soul the best delight that may
  Encheer it most, and most our spirits inflame
To thoughts of glory, and to worthy ends.

In 1605 Daniel published a short but unusually sprightly lyric in dialogue, called *Ulysses and the Siren.*

The plays of Daniel, as Mr. Saintsbury has noted, occupy the curious position of being the only English tragedies of the age "distinctly couched in the form of the Seneca model," which was so abundantly employed in France. But we can scarcely dwell upon them here, since *Cleopatra* was already printed in 1594, and *Philotas*, though not published until 1605, was unquestionably written, in the main, at least three years before the death of Elizabeth. The four masques or entertainments of Daniel remain, as distinctly Jacobean work, to be considered. The *Vision of the Twelve Goddesses*, 1604, shows a hand unaccustomed to these trifles, and is not a little dull. Much more skilful and poetical is *The Queen's Arcadia*, 1605, which is entirely in verse, blank and rhymed, inextricably interwoven ; this is rather a romantic tragi-comedy in five acts, than

a masque.   *Tethys's Festival,* 1610, on the other hand,
preserves the conventional forms of that kind of enter-
tainment.   It contains this song, very characteristic of
Daniel's delicate manner of moralizing—

> Are they shadows that we see?
>   And can shadows pleasure give?
> Pleasures only pleasures be
>   Cast by bodies we conceive,
> And are made the things we deem,
> In those figures which are seen.
>
> But these pleasures vanish fast,
>   Which by shadows are exprest ;
> Pleasures are not if they last,
>   In their passing is their best ;
> Glory is most bright and gay,
> In a flash, and so away.
>
> Feed apace, then, greedy eyes,
>   On the wonder you behold ;
> Take it sudden as it flies,
>   Though you take it not to hold ;
> When your eyes have done their part,
> Thought must length it in the heart.

Hymen's Triumph, 1615, like *The Queen's Arcadia,* is
a species of pastoral tragi-comedy, languid in action, but
very exactly versified.   This piece was highly praised
by Coleridge, who was a great admirer of the author.
" Read Daniel," he said, " the admirable Daniel ; " but
in the pleasure he took in his limpidity it is possible that
Coleridge underrated the aridity of the laureate.   The
almost unrelieved excision of all ornament and colour,
the uniform stateliness, the lack of passion, which render
Daniel admirable and sometimes even charming in a

short poem, weary us in his long productions, and so invariably sententious is he that we are tempted to call him a Polonius among poets.

Another transitional figure is that of Joshua Sylvester, whom few historians of literature have deigned to mention. He was, however, an active producer of successful verse in his own age, and he wielded, moreover, by means of his famous translation, a prodigious influence. He was born in 1563, in Kent. As early as 1591 he began that version of the *Divine Weeks and Works* of the French poet, Du Bartas, by which he is principally known. He had the custom, fortunately very unusual at that time, of not dating his title-pages, so that his bibliography is particularly obscure ; but he seems to have gone on publishing, revising, and reprinting until close upon his death in 1618. For the last six years of his life he lived at Middelburg, in Holland, as the secretary to the Company of Merchant Venturers there. The particular fate, therefore, which he had most bitterly dreaded and deprecated fell upon him, for his fear had always been to die in exile. Into his translation of Du Bartas he had interpolated this appeal—

> Ah, courteous England, thy kind arms I see,
> Wide-stretchèd out to save and welcome me.
> Thou, tender mother, wilt not suffer age,
> To snow my locks in foreign pilgrimage,
> That fell Brazil my breathless corpse should shroud,
> Or golden Peru of my praise be proud,
> Or rich Cathay to glory in my verse ;
> Thou gav'st me cradle ; thou wilt give my hearse ?

But the prayer was unheard.

Sylvester was ambitious of high distinction, but he was

dragged down by poverty and by a natural turbidity of style. His original sonnets and lyrics are constantly striking, but never flawless; his translations, as poems, are full of force and colour, but crude. His talent was genuine, but it never ripened, and seems to be turning sour when it should be growing mellow. He does not fear to be tiresome and grotesque for pages at a time, and in Du Bartas he unhappily found a model who, in spite of his own remarkable qualities, sanctioned the worst errors of Sylvester. Milton was, however, attracted to Du Bartas, and approached him, almost unquestionably, through Sylvester, whose version was extremely popular until the middle of the century. Sylvester's vocabulary was very extensive, and he revelled in the pseudo-scientific phraseology of his French prototype.

Nicholas Breton was an Elizabethan primitive, who went on publishing fresh volumes until after the death of James I., but without having modified the sixteenth-century character of his style. He was probably born in 1542, and lived on till 1626. His books are very numerous, most of them, however, being mere pamphlets. He wrote indifferently in prose and verse. The most notable of his little volumes of poetry first published during the reign of James, are *The Passionate Shepherd*, 1604; *The Honour of Valour*, 1605; and *I would and yet I would not*, 1614; the larger part of Breton's Jacobean work being in prose.

Of these short productions *The Passionate Shepherd* is by far the best, and ranks very high among Breton's contributions to poetry. It is a collection of pastoral

lyrics, in a variety of measures, very lightly, liquidly, and
innocently thrown off, with no sense of intellectual effort
and no great attention to style. Breton has a very
pleasant acquaintance with nature, and can bring up
before us such charming pictures as enable us to

> See the fishes leap and play,
> In a blessèd sunny day ;
> Or to hear the partridge call,
> Till she have her covey all ;
> Or to see the subtle fox,
> How the villain flies the box,
> After feeding on his prey ;
> How he closely sneaks away,
> Through the hedge and down the furrow,
> Till he gets into his burrow ;
> Then the bee to gather honey ;
> And the little black-haired coney,
> On the bank for sunny place,
> With her forefeet wash her face.

There is humour and ingenuity in his *I would and yet
I would not*, a long statement of the attractions and
the disadvantage of almost every walk of life, contrasted
in this manner—

> I would I were a keeper of a park,
>   To walk with my bent cross-bow and my hound,
> To know my game, and closely in the dark
>   To lay a barren doe upon the ground,
> And by my venison, more than by my fees,
> To feed on better meat than bread and cheese.
>
> And yet I would not ; lest, if I be spied,
>   I might be turnèd quite out of my walk,
> And afterwards more punishment abide,
>   Than 'longs unto a little angry talk,
> And cause more mischief after all come to me,
> Than all the good the does did ever do me.

This is picturesque ; but the see-saw becomes tedious when extended over more than one hundred and fifty stanzas. Breton had the root of poetry in him, but he was no scholar, inartistic, and absolutely devoid of the gift of self-criticism. A small posy has been selected by Mr. Bullen from the wilderness of his overgrown garden.

A similar writer, of perhaps as great general talent, but not so true a poet, was Samuel Rowlands. He was probably thirty years Breton's junior, and did not begin to write until within a few years of the death of Elizabeth. He passes out of our sight in 1630. His works consist of satirical characters in verse, mainly in the six-line stanza, describing those fantastical types of the day which so many of the minor writers delighted in caricaturing. They are often well-written, clear, pointed, and regular, never rising to the incisive melody of a great poet, but never sinking below a fairly admirable level, while for the student of manners they abound in realistic detail. Some of the most amusing of these collections come before our period, but *Look to it, or I'll stab you,* 1604, is as good as any of its predecessors. *A Terrible Battle between Fire and Death,* 1606, aims, not wholly without success, at nobler things, but becomes tedious and grotesque.

As time went on, Rowlands' verse grew less senten-tious, and more broadly farcical, and *The Whole Crew of Kind Gossips,* 1609, is a favourable example of his " new humour." As we review his successive volumes, we find but slight further change, except that they grow a little coarser and heavier. *The Melancholy Knight,* 1615,

is the best of his later productions. In all the verse of
Rowlands we meet with the same qualities, a low and
trivial view of life, an easy satire, a fluency and purity of
language which never reaches elevation of style. A dull
book of sacred prose and poetry, called *Heaven's Glory,
Seek It,* 1628, closes the long catalogue of the writings
of Rowlands.

When we turn to the dramatists, we meet at once with
one name which, while it is mainly the glory of Elizabeth,
belongs in part to the reign of her successor. It would
be ridiculous, in this place, to attempt the smallest
critical consideration of Shakespeare's writings, or even of
that fourth part of them which may be thought of as
Jacobean. I shall therefore confine myself to a bare
statement of the latest opinion with regard to what plays
were composed after the accession of James I., and in
what form these were published. Just before the death
of Elizabeth, as is generally admitted, a great change
came over the temper of Shakespeare, and led him to
the composition of his series of lofty tragedies of passion.
To these succeeded, five or six years later, the quartet of
splendid romances with which his dramatic activity seems
to close, since, later than 1611, we can scarcely with any
certitude detect him actively at work.

Among the plays belonging to our time, *Hamlet* can
hardly be included, for there can be little doubt that it
was written in its present form, and ready for the press,
in July, 1602, when *The Revenge of Hamlet, Prince of
Denmark,* was entered in the Stationers' Registers. It
was not printed, however, until 1603, in an edition of
which but two copies survive, both imperfect. By that

time it had been acted by the King's Players, and " in
the two Universities of Oxford and Cambridge." In
this edition of 1603 Polonius is named Corambis, and
there are certain very feeble passages which do not occur
again.   It has been supposed that these are remnants of
the pre-Shakespearean *Hamlet,* with which it is now
considered improbable that the great poet had any connection previous to 1602, when it was doubtless re-
modelled by him for the stage.   Five quarto editions
appeared during Shakespeare's lifetime.

The date of *King Lear* is pretty well ascertained.   It
must have been written after the publication of Dr.
Harsnet's book in 1603, and before it was entered in the
Stationers' Registers at Christmas, 1606.   An attempt
has been made, founded on the phrase, " I smell the
blood of a British man," and other slight internal
evidence, to tie the date of composition still more
tightly down to the close of 1604 and opening of 1605.
This is a highly probable hypothesis, but one which
cannot, in the present state of our knowledge, be insisted
on.   There was printed in 1594 a chronicle-history of
Lear, King of England, but this has disappeared, and
we do not even know whether it was a play.   A drama
of that name, however, was issued in 1605, when the
Lear of Shakespeare was probably already written ; it is
of no great merit, and bears little resemblance to the
real tragedy, of which two editions were published early
in 1608.

The early editors of Shakespeare, and Malone during
his lifetime, declared *Othello* to have been written in
1611.   But Malone, in a posthumous publication,

positively revised this date, and gave 1604, saying, "we
know it was acted in" that year. What was the source
of Malone's information is uncertain, but it tallies with
a mysterious entry in the Revels Book, which itself is
forged, but which seems to have been copied from a
genuine document, now lost, once accessible to Malone.
Othello was not printed until 1622, a year before the
first folio.

To the dramas we have enumerated some degree
of date-certainty is afforded by the fact that they appeared in quarto form. *Troilus and Cressida*, too,
which may or may not have been in existence in 1603,
was published in 1609. But of the eight magnificent
performances which must now be mentioned no edition
is known to exist earlier than the folio of 1623,
and the dates of their being written are therefore very
difficult to conjecture with assurance. It is, however,
certain that *Antony and Cleopatra* was entered in the
Stationers' Registers in May, 1608, and it was probably
written during the preceding year. There is absolutely
no evidence regarding *Timon of Athens* and *Coriolanus*,
but the years 1607 and 1608 are usually assigned to
them. *Cymbeline* was possibly composed in 1609, or in
1610 at the latest. Dr. Simon Forman saw *Macbeth*
acted at the Globe on the 20th of April, 1610, and
The Tempest, apparently, in the course of the same year;
he saw *The Winter's Tale* on the 15th of May, 1611,
and these plays were, on these occasions, it is probable,
of recent composition. This chronological arrangement
is borne out by the changes in the structure of Shakespeare's verse, changes to which a too mechanical im-

portance has been assigned, but which are none the less of positive value in the consideration of the succession of his plays. *Pericles* was published in quarto-form in 1609, and was doubtless written during the preceding year, when George Wilkins, who is believed to have collaborated on it with Shakespeare, brought out his prose tale in illustration of the plot of the play. Finally, it may be noted that the Sonnets, which, apparently, were not completed until 1605, first saw the light in the quarto of 1609.

In the course of his elaborate monograph on the writings of the author of *Old Fortunatus*, Mr. Swinburne has confessed that " of all English poets, if not of all poets on record, Dekker is perhaps the most difficult to classify." This is in part due to the excessive redundancy with which he flung unacknowledged fragments of his work hither and thither, a father without a trace of parental instinct. Thomas Dekker was born, doubtless of Dutch parentage in London, about 1567, and did not begin to work until about 1590. Yet, before Elizabeth died, he was the author of eight plays of his own, and in nearly thirty he had combined with others. Of this mass of dramatic production the greater part has disappeared. During the Jacobean period he continued to write in the same casual way, ready to throw in his lot with anybody, but rarely producing a drama entirely by himself. He gradually turned away more and more from verse, and became famous as a pamphleteer and author of sensational tracts. He disappeared about 1632.

The best of his plays is probably one in which he allied himself with Middleton in 1604, a second part appearing several years later.   In this occurs the famous passage about patience, which has been universally attributed to Dekker—

> Patience ! why, 'tis the soul of peace :
> Of all the virtues, 'tis nearest kin to heaven ;
> It makes men look like gods.   The best of men
> That e'er wore earth about him was a sufferer,
> A soft, meek, patient, humble, tranquil spirit ;
> The first true gentleman that ever breathed.

The delicately humorous character of Orlando Friscobaldo is an example of work excellently done in a class rarely attempted by Dekker, who is unrivalled in short pathetic scenes, has a tenderness that is all his own, combines with a sweet fancy a rare lyrical gift, but is excessively unequal as a craftsman, and mars some of his finest efforts by his impatience, his incoherence, and his carelessness.   It is difficult to understand how it can be possible that the author of the detestable stuff called *If it be not good, the Devil is in it,* could have turned away to contribute to Massinger's *Virgin Martyr* the exquisite episode between the heroine and the angel. This extravagant inequality, ever recurring, creates the standing difficulty about the literary position of Dekker.

John Marston is believed to have lived on until 1634, but his dramatic activity was almost entirely confined to the four last years of the reign of Elizabeth.   In the first year of James I. he seems to have composed his *Parasitaster,* and to have resigned *The Insatiate Countess* into the hands of Barkstead to arrange and complete. Some trifling pageants and entertainments close his work, but Marston is to be considered as essentially Elizabethan.

CHAPTER II.

THE death of Elizabeth was a turning-point in the life of Ben Jonson. When James I. came to the throne of England, there were few among the poets whom he welcomed with greater geniality than the rough young man of thirty, hitherto scarcely known except for a series of dramatic satires, and for a quarrelsomeness of temper which had led him into several ugly scrapes. He was selected for a new trade, that of masque-maker, and in June, 1603, he gratified the queen and Prince Henry by presenting *The Satyr* before them at Althorpe. The success of this exquisite trifle decided in part Ben Jonson's vocation. For the rest of James's reign, in spite of Daniel's and Dekker's jealousy, he was the favourite arranger of this class of entertainments. Busy as he was, however, with his duties as court poet, he found time before the close of 1603 to write *Sejanus his Fall*, the earliest of his Roman tragedies. In this play Shakespeare acted, and, according to the general belief, added considerably to the acting version. When Ben Jonson, however, printed *Sejanus*, in 1605, he omitted all Shakespeare's lines, rather " than to defraud so happy a

genius of his right by my loathed usurpation." He got
into trouble with Lord Northampton over *Sejanus*, and
was imprisoned in company with Chapman. In 1605
Chapman and Jonson were once more in " a vile prison "
for writing against the Scotch in *Eastward Hoe !* It was
on the occasion of their release that that Roman matron,
the mother of Ben, so distinguished herself. " After their
delivery, he banqueted all his friends ; there was Camden,
Selden, and others. At the midst of the feast, his old
mother drank to him, and showed him a paper which
she had (if the sentence had taken execution) to have
mixed in the prison among his drink, which was full of
lusty strong poison ; and, that she was no churl, she told,
she minded first to have drunk of it herself."

Late in 1605 Ben Jonson added a cubit to his literary
stature by producing his noble comedy of *Volpone or the
Fox.* All these years he was not merely a frequenter of
the wits' meeting at the Mermaid Tavern in Friday Street,
but the very centre and main attraction of the club. In
1609 his comedy of *Epicene, or the Silent Woman,* was
brought out, and in 1610 *The Alchymist.* This was Ben
Jonson's blossoming-time, and everything he now did
was admirable. A second Roman tragedy, *Catiline,*
dates from 1611. Ben Jonson, who had been a Roman
Catholic, presently embraced the Protestant faith, and,
very shortly after, Sir Walter Raleigh selected him as
travelling-companion to his young son Walter, who was
"knavishly inclined." The poet continued for some
time to be bear-leader to this youth, and seems, while in
Paris, to have interpreted the anxious father's directions
somewhat lazily. There was a break here in the incessant

succession of Jonson's masques, and his next play was *Bartholomew Fair*, acted late in 1614. On the 1st of February, 1616, the king appointed Ben Jonson his poet-laureate, with a salary of a hundred marks a year, and after bringing out *The Devil's an Ass*, the playwright ceased for a while from his dramatic labours. In 1616 he published a folio collection of his works, which contained not only the plays, which had already appeared successively in quarto, but five new masques, several entertainments, a sheaf of epigrams, and the lyrical and occasional pieces known as *The Forest*.

The life of Jonson for the next few years is rather obscure. In the summer of 1618 he travelled on foot to Scotland, and remained away for about six months. In the first days of 1619, he paid his celebrated visit to Drummond at Hawthornden. Immediately after his departure, Drummond took the copious notes of Jonson's conversation, which are among the most precious relics of the age that we possess. The greatest nonsense has been talked about the "malice" and "perfidy" of the Scotch poet. No charge could be less deserved. An exceedingly interesting guest had been speaking to him with absolute freedom about that literary life of London, in which Drummond took an acute and somewhat wistful interest. Nothing could be more natural, and nothing for us more fortunate, than that the host, when Jonson had departed, should jot down what the guest had said. Drummond has shown great art in his notes; we seem to hear the very voice of Jonson. The latter returned to England, and found himself welcome at court, but we know little of his avocations there. In earlier years he had worked with the celebrated architect Inigo Jones, with whom he had collaborated in the masques of *Blackness* in 1605, *Hymen* in 1606, and *Queens* in 1609. Jones had been abroad in France and Italy, but returned to be the Royal Surveyor in 1615. In Ben Jonson and Inigo Jones, two headstrong wills met in conflict, and the poet told Prince Charles " that when he wanted words to express the greatest villain in the world he would call him an Inigo." At last, after ten years, the two great inventors became friends again in 1622, when they combined in the masque of *Time Vindicated* (January, 1623), and they remained on terms of mutual toleration till 1631. Meanwhile, in October, 1623, there occurred the disastrous fire in Jonson's house, which is described in his poem, *An Execration upon Vulcan ;* in this many of the poet's manuscripts, and perhaps a play, were destroyed. Just before the death of the king, Jonson produced another drama, *The Staple of News*, in 1625.

Early in 1626 the poet, who was worn with labours, rather than years, suffered from a stroke of paralysis, and another followed in 1628. But in September of the latter year, having recovered health, he was able to succeed Thomas Middleton, the dramatist, as City Chronologer. In 1629 was " negligently played," and "squeamishly censured," the comedy of *The New Inn*, published in 1631 ; the epilogue tells us that " the maker is sick and sad." Ben Jonson arraigned the reception of this play, by writing an arrogant *Ode to Himself*, which created a considerable sensation, and was parodied or answered, in a tone uniformly flattering and gracious,

by several of the young generation of poets, to whom
Jonson was now an object of veneration.   In 1631, on
occasion of the publication of certain masques, the old
quarrel between Ben Jonson and Inigo Jones broke out
again.   Jonson was extremely violent, lost his position
at court, and was superseded by Carew and Aurelian
Townsend.   Another comedy, *The Magnetic Lady*, was
licensed in 1632, but so unsuccessfully acted that it
was not published till 1641.   The old unprinted play of
A Tale of a Tub, which Mr. Fleay attributes to 1601,
was revised in 1634, but all these late performances were
complete failures, and Jonson broke down under such
a mountain of misfortunes.   He does not seem to have
been in want during his latest years, and the young men
of promise surrounded him and lavished their honours
upon him.   But he was sick and dejected, and without
any philosophy to support him.   He died on the 6th of
August, 1637, at the age of sixty-four, and was buried
three days later in Westminster Abbey.   Rare Ben
Jonson !

By universal consent, the three great comedies of
Jonson's central period are his masterpieces.   Coleridge
could never be sure whether it was *Volpone* or *The Alchymist* which he thought the first of English comedies.   Mr.
Swinburne has expressed the general opinion of lovers
of poetry when he says that "no other of even Jonson's
greatest works is at once so admirable and so enjoy-
able" as *Volpone*, grounding this judgment on the existence in that play of something imaginative and even
romantic, which is wanting in *The Alchymist.*   The
hero, Volpone, is a Venetian magnifico who feigns

sickness and the approach of death, that, like a fox,
he may delude those who gather round him, and may
observe them at his leisure.   He is an amateur of
covetousness, and it is his passion to fill his palace,
like a museum, with specimens of the greedy and the
obsequious.   But Volpone is much more than a mere
hunter after oddities; he is himself the most glorious
living example of the vice that he imputes.   But he
possesses wealth to excess, and though at the opening
of the play we find him brooding in an ecstasy over piles
of gold, plate and jewels, what now renders him the
keenest pleasure is to see other men and women fawn-
ing upon him, in hope of soon dividing his possessions.
Three types of legacy-hunters are introduced, Voltore,
Corbaccio, and Corvino, each a shrewd rogue, but all
easily gulled by the superior cunning of the fox.   It is
needless to tell the story of the plot, which contains one
agreeable female character, Celia, and in the young
Bonario one man of honour.   All critics have united in
praising the solidity of the architecture which has built
up this splendid edifice of satire, and placed upon it the
tower or spire of its glittering fifth act, in which, lest
the strain of our indignation should be too great, a fitting
retribution is allowed to fall upon fox alike and the
seeming-successful jackal that has waited upon and
betrayed him.

In construction *The Alchymist* is perhaps finer still,
and remains, in spite of its proved unfittedness for the
stage, and its antiquated interests, one of the most
splendid compositions written by an English hand.
Lamb, with unerring instinct, hit upon the central jewel

of the whole splendid fabric when he selected for special
praise the long scene in Subtle's house, where Epicure
Mammon boasts what rare things he will do when he
obtains the philosopher's stone.   Here Jonson, running
and leaping under the tremendous weight of his own
equipment, perfectly overwhelms the judgment "by the
torrent of images, words, and book-knowledge with which
Mammon confounds and stuns" us.   In *The Alchymist*
the voluptuousness of avarice, rather than its cruelty or
cunning, occupies the poet's pencil.   The borderland of
tragedy is not here approached, as it was in the deeper
savagery of *Volpone.*   Neither Subtle, Face, nor Dol is
other than a tame or farcical rogue by the side of the
horrors who succeeded one another by the Fox's mock
deathbed.   But the intrigue is much more ingenious and
yet reasonable in the later than in the earlier play, and
indeed in mere strength and originality of elaborate invention no play ever written exceeded *The Alchymist.*
Here, again, the winding-up of the plot is of the first
order of felicitous art.

The only charge, indeed, which can be brought against
either of these magnificent and stately comedies is
that art rules in them to the dispossession of nature.
An intellectual cause determines the position of every
scene, almost of every line.   An emotional irregularity,
proof of a less crystalline perfection of workmanship,
would be welcomed by the reader, and while criticism
can scarcely modify its praise of those two comedies,
the heart is not touched in them, and their study but
proves the curious figures which move so ingeniously in
them to have been invented in the closet, not observed

in the street. There is infinite wit and intelligence expended, but upon a scene which is never a reflection of life itself.

Between the comedies came *The Silent Woman*, which is commonly named with them. But this is a work of inferior merit. It is a charming farce, but we cannot, as Dryden did, "prefer it before all other plays, as I do its author, in judgment, above all other poets." The eccentric Morose cannot endure the least noise in his house, and has never married, because he fears the loud clack of a woman's tongue. His nephew, Dauphine, produces a girl, Epicene, who never speaks above a whisper, nor otherwise than in monosyllables. But on the wedding-day the bride pours forth a perfect cascade of conversation, deafening the unhappy bridegroom, and it is only when he is reduced to the verge of despair, that his wicked nephew confesses to him that the marriage was void, and the Silent Woman a boy dressed up in girl's clothes. The general character of this lively play oddly resembles the lighter forms of comedy which, after the example of Molière, were, sixty years later, to invade the English stage.

The other plays of Ben Jonson which came within the Jacobean period are of inferior interest; but the poet's attempt to teach Roman history by means of stiff blank-verse tragedies must not be overlooked. Coleridge wished that we had more than two of these Roman pieces, but the wish is one which it is hard to echo. Mr. Swinburne has excellently remarked, and it is peculiarly true of *Sejanus* and *Catiline*, that Ben Jonson "took so much interest in the creations that he had none left for the

creatures of his intellect or art." The personages are
drawn with extreme elaboration, and everything which
is recorded of them by Sallust or Tacitus, even to their
most trifling utterances, is woven into the dialogue; but
the dramatist never lets himself go, and never breathes
the breath of life into the Frankenstein monsters of his
learned fancy. At the same time, the art of Jonson is
very purely displayed in these stiff tragedies. The verse
marches with a certain heavy grandeur; the language is
as stately as the sentiments and imagery are magnificent.
A studied prosiness, doubtless affected to protest against
the purple patchiness of the school of Marlowe, affects
the entire composition, and makes the continuous reading
of these Roman plays a tedious exercise.

Catiline's Conspiracy has the same faults, to greater
excess. Certain parts of this tragedy—such as the long
soliloquy of the Ghost of Sylla in Catiline's study, and the
death-scene of the hero—are perhaps more striking as
poetry than anything in *Sejanus;* but the later play is
even more bombastic, wooden, and undramatic than the
earlier. Choruses are introduced, in the manner of
Seneca, but not felicitously. One in the second act,
however, applauding the ancient virtue of the citizen, has
a fine ring—

> Such were the great Camilli too,
> 　The Fabii, Scipios ; that still thought
> 　No work at price enough was bought,
> That for their country they could do.
>
> And to her honour did so knit,
> 　As all their acts were understood,
> 　The sinews of the public good ;
> And they themselves one soul with it.

> These men were truly magistrates,
>> These neither practised force nor forms ;
>> Nor did they leave the helm in storms ;
> And such they are make happy states.

Among the works which follow the great comedies the surprising farce of *Bartholomew Fair,* crowded with personages, takes a foremost rank. Here, with an astounding vitality, Jonson surrounds the conception of Roast Pig with a riot of contrasted figures, shouting, struggling, permeating the Fair with their superabundant animation. There is no dramatic work in English at all comparable in its own kind with this brilliant and be-wildering presentment of a comic turmoil, and, by a curious chance, it is exactly here, where it might be expected that the dramatist would be peculiarly tempted to subordinate all attempt at character-painting to the mere embodiment of humours, that one of Ben Jonson's few really living and breathing creatures is found in the person of the Puritan, Rabbi Zeal-of-the-Land. But after 1615 the dramatic genius of Jonson underwent a sort of ossification, and few readers are able greatly to enjoy his later plays. Dryden roundly styled them all his " dotages," and it is certain that, although special study may discover beauties in each of them, the merits of Ben Jonson's style are seen to dwindle, and his faults to become more patent. There is certainly a want of interest and coherence in *The Devil is an Ass!* and though Mr. Swinburne, whose authority is not lightly to be put aside, claims special appreciation for the Aristo-phanic comedy of *The Staple of News,* it has not the charm of Ben Jonson's earlier plays. The romantic

comedies of *The New Inn* and the *Magnetic Lady*, and the
confused, boorish farce of *The Tale of a Tub*, possess the
unmistakable features of Ben Jonson's style, but the life
has evaporated, and has left only the skeleton of his too
elaborate and self-conscious artistic system.

Two examples of the dramatic blank verse of Ben
Jonson may suffice to give a taste of his style.   The
first is a speech of Latiaris in the fourth act of *Sejanus*—

> Methinks the genius of the Roman race
> Should not be so extinct, but that bright flame
> Of liberty might be revived again
> (Which no good man but with his life should lose),
> And we not sit like spent and patient fools,
> Still puffing in the dark at one poor coal,
> Held on by hope till the last spark is out.
> The cause is public, and the honour, name,
> The immortality of every soul,
> That is not bastard or a slave in Rome,
> Therein concerned ; whereto, if men would change
> The wearied arm, and for the weighty shield
> So long sustained, employ the facile sword,
> We might have soon assurance of our vows.
> This ass's fortitude doth tire us all :
> It must be active valour must redeem
> Our loss, or none.   The rock and our hard steel
> Should meet to enforce those glorious fires again,
> Whose splendour cheered the world, and heat gave life
> No less than doth the sun's.

The other is the magnificent burst of Sir Epicure
Mammon's, with which the second act of the *Alchymist*
opens—

> Come on, sir !   Now you set your foot on shore
> In Novo Orbe ; here's the rich Peru ;
> And there within, sir, are the golden mines,
> Great Solomon's Ophir !   He was sailing to it

Three years, but we have reached it in ten months.
This is the day on which, to all my friends,
I will pronounce the happy word, *Be rich ;*
This day you shall be spectatissimi.
You shall no more deal with the hollow die,
Or the frail card. . . . No more
Shall thirst of satin, or the covetous hunger
Of velvet entrails for a rude-spun cloak,
To be displayed at Madam Augusta's, make
The sons of Sword and Hazard fall before
The golden calf, and, on their knees, whole nights,
Commit idolatry with wine and trumpets,
Or go a feasting after drum and ensign ;
No more of this!

A very large section of Ben Jonson's work consists of his masques and entertainments, to which he gave a great part of his best ingenuity for twenty years. It was long held that these pieces were devoid of merit, and that the poet debased his genius in consenting to write them. Even Malone spoke of them as "bungling shows," in which "the wretched taste of those times found amusement." But the taste of our own day has reverted in many respects to that of the early seventeenth century, and now each successive critic speaks with greater admiration of the masques of Ben Jonson. The masque was a developed pageant, into which music and poetry had been imported to give a greater richness and fulness to the design. It had been conveyed into England from Italy early in the sixteenth century, but it was not until Ben Jonson took it in hand that it became noticeable as a branch of literary art. Serious as was the bent of his intellect, he did not disdain these elegant and charming diversions. He believed himself capable of rendering

them immortal by his verse, and in the preface to one of
them, the *Hymenaei* of 1606, he says as much ; he claims
to have given to the masque that intellectual vitality
without which "the glory of these solemnities had
perished like a blaze, and gone out in the beholders'
eyes." He was right ; for if we are familiar with the
masques of James and Anne, and have forgotten the
very names of those performed in honour of their predecessors, it is the literary art of Jonson and Daniel and
Campion which has preserved alive for us what the
skill of the architect, musician, milliner, and scene-painter
could not contrive to immortalize.

The most valuable part of these once gorgeous masques
is therefore, of course, the lyrical verse fantastically
strewn throughout them. This is of very various
interest, some of it stiff and occasional, rough with
oddities which no longer appeal to us, wanting in
suavity and sweetness ; much of it, on the other hand,
extremely delicate, surprising, and aerial. Sometimes,
with his allusions and the copious learning of his notes,
Ben Jonson turns a masque into a work of positive
weight. *The Masque of Queens,* for instance, is an
important poem on the subject of witchcraft, treated
with exhaustive picturesqueness.

The song which introduces the dance in *Pleasure
Reconciled to Virtue,* 1619, is a happy example of Jonson's
skill in the lyrical part of these entertainments—

> Come on, come on ! and, where you go,
>   So interweave the curious knot,
> As even the observer scarce may know
>   Which lives are Pleasure's, and which not.

First figure out the doubtful way,
At which awhile all youth should stay,
Where she and Virtue did contend
Which should have Hercules to friend.

Then as all actions of mankind
    Are but a labyrinth or maze,
So let your dances be entwined ;
    Yet not perplex men into gaze ;

But measured, and so numerous too,
As men may read each act they do ;
And when they see the graces meet,
Admire the wisdom of your feet.

For dancing is an exercise,
    Not only shows the mover's wit,
But maketh the beholder wise,
    As he hath power to rise to it.

James I.'s taste for masques gave the poet great scope for a liberal invention. It is said that the king spent £4000 in this way during the seven first years of his reign, for he and the queen each presented a masque at Christmas and at Shrovetide.

In *The Sad Shepherd*, a pastoral fragment not published until 1641, Jonson attempted a higher species of enter-tainment; so far as we are able to judge, he had formed a false idea of the shape a bucolic drama should take, but the truncated scenes of *The Sad Shepherd* contain some beautiful writing. The opening lines form the most delicate example of his skill in blank verse which has come down to us—

Here was she wont to go ! and here ! and here !
Just where these daisies, pinks, and violets grow ;
The world may find the spring by following her ;

For other print her airy steps ne'er left.
Her treading would not bend a blade of grass,
Or shake the downy blow-ball from his stalk !
But like the soft west wind she shot along,
And where she went, the flowers took thickest root.

The miscellaneous poems of Ben Jonson present features of peculiar interest, but they are of the most bewildering inequality of merit. His *Epigrams* are not merely exceedingly bad in themselves, but they led to the formation of numberless imitations, and a baleful department of seventeenth-century literature. It is not to be wondered at that Sir Walter Scott should rise from the perusal of these nasty little pieces with the conviction that Jonson enjoyed "using the language of scavengers and nightmen." We turn with relief to *The Forest*, a collection of fifteen poems, mainly elegiacal, all of a high level of merit, all distinguished and vigorous, although none, perhaps, of superlative beauty. All Ben Jonson's other miscellanies find themselves jumbled together under the heading of *Underwoods*. Among these are to be found many copies of verses which are interesting as the work of so great a man, some which, though always rather stiff, are elegant and pleasing in themselves, and a majority which not even the vast prestige of Ben can induce us to read with enjoyment or even with toleration. The graces of the Jacobean age were rarely at the beck of Ben Jonson, and when he does not succeed in his own elaborate way, he ceases to succeed at all.

The genius of Ben Jonson was long regarded with a sort of superstitious reverence. Even Dryden, who was the first to question his supremacy, admitted that he thought Ben Jonson "the most learned and judicious writer which any theatre ever had," and acknowledged him "the more correct poet," but Shakespeare "the greater wit." Although such language would now be held extravagant, and although Jonson is not any longer mentioned among English writers of the very first rank, he retains a firm and important place in our literature. Incongruous as his works are, and much as his style lacks fidelity to any particular ideal, the image we form of the poetry of Jonson is a very definite and a very striking one. He called those "works" which others call "plays," as Sir John Suckling complained, and everywhere we find him laborious, strenuous, and solid. His writings give us the impression of a very bold piece of composite architecture, by no means pure in style, and constructed after a fashion no longer admired, nor naturally suitable to the climate, but rich, stately, and imposing.

The character of the man is clearly reflected in Jonson's writings, and forms by no means their least interesting feature. They, like the fierce bricklayer's son, like the guest of Drummond and the enemy of Inigo Jones, like the master of "the mountain belly and the rocky face," are truculent, saturnine, direct, full of arrogance and sincerity, permeated with a love of literature, but without human passion or tenderness. In spite of the fabulous wealth of imagination and eloquence which lie close below the surface of Ben Jonson's works, few indeed are those who dig there for treasure. He repels his admirers, he holds readers at arm's length. He is the least sympathetic of all the great English poets, and to appreciate him the rarest of literary tastes is required,— an appetite for dry intellectual beauty, for austerity of thought, for poetry that is logical, and hard, and lusty. Yet he did a mighty work for the English language. At a time when it threatened to sink into mere prettiness or oddity, and to substitute what was non-essential for what was definite and durable, Jonson threw his massive learning and logic into the scale, and forbade Jacobean poetry to kick the beam. He was rewarded by the passionate devotion of a tribe of wits and scholars; he made a deep mark on our literature for several generations subsequent to his own, and he enjoys the perennial respect of all close students of poetry.

A name which it is natural to think of in conjunction with Jonson's is that of George Chapman, who resembled him in the austerity of his judgment, in his devotion to the classics, and in his distinguished attitude to letters. But while Jonson was a noble dramatist and a very bad translator, Chapman was one of the best translators that England has ever produced, and, if I may venture to state a personal conviction, a dramatist whose merits were exceedingly scanty. This latter opinion is one which it may perhaps seem foolhardy to express, for Lamb, who first drew attention to his plays, has praised them exuberantly, and Mr. Swinburne has done Chapman the honour of dedicating to a study of his works a considerable volume, to which all careful readers must be recommended. That no injustice should be done here to this poet, I will at once record the fact that Lamb has said, " Of all the English playwriters, Chapman

perhaps approaches nearest to Shakespeare in the
descriptive and didactic, in passages which are less
purely dramatic." It is rash to differ from Lamb, but
I am bound in mere sincerity to admit that I find
nothing even remotely Shakespearian in plays that seem
bombastic, loose, and incoherent to the last extreme, and
in which the errors of the primitive Elizabethans, due
mainly to inexperience, are complacently repeated and
continued through the noblest years of perfected art,
in which Shakespeare, Jonson, and Fletcher held the
stage. Chapman was an admirable and sometimes even
a great poet, but it is hard to admit that he was
ever a tolerable playwright.

George Chapman was born at Hitchin about 1559, and
was therefore past middle life when James I. ascended
the throne of England. He was educated at Oxford,
but we know absolutely nothing about his occupations
until he was nearly forty years of age. In the last years
of Elizabeth he came to London, and was engaged in
dramatic work from about 1595 to 1608. We know of
eight or nine plays produced before the death of the
queen, five of which have survived. His Jacobean
dramas are *Monsieur d'Olive*, published in 1606, but
acted earlier ; *Bussy d'Ambois*, printed 1607 ; *Eastward
Hoe !* of which mention has been already made, in which
Chapman collaborated in 1605, with Jonson and
Marston ; *The Widow's Tears*, acted about the same
time, but not published until 1612 ; *The Revenge of
Bussy d'Ambois*, printed in 1613, but acted much earlier ;
Byron's Conspiracy and *Byron's Tragedy*, each of 1608.
As late as 1631, there was published a tragedy of *Cæsar*

and Pompey, evidently an old rejected play of Chapman's youth. With these exceptions, and those of two tragic fragments which Shirley found, completed and published in the next age, all Chapman's dramatic work may be safely consigned to the age of Elizabeth.

Webster commended Chapman more highly than any of his contemporaries, or, at least, in enumerating them mentioned his name first, and expressed his warm appreciation of "that full and heightened style" in which he considered Chapman's tragedies to be written. Such praise, from such a man, may not lightly be passed over; yet Chapman's last and most friendly apologist finds himself forced to admit that "the height indeed is somewhat giddy, and the fulness too often tends or threatens to dilate into tumidity." Of the four French tragedies, *Bussy d'Ambois* is undoubtedly the most interesting, being full of soliloquies and declamatory passages that have a true ring of epic poetry about them, and being at least as nearly allied to a play as the essentially undramatic mind of Chapman could make it. Of the comedies two are certainly readable : *Monsieur d'Olive*, a whirligig of fashionable humours and base love, is undoubtedly put together with a good deal of spirit and some humour, and *May Day*, a "coil to make wit and women friends," is a still madder piece of extravagance.

But even these prose plays, certainly the most coherent and amusing evidences of Chapman's talent as a dramatist, are in no sense thoroughly satisfactory. The estimate of women throughout is base to the last degree ; no dramatist of the period satirizes the other sex with such malignant and persistent sarcasm as Chapman. It is a point that seriously militates against any claim he may put forward to greatness, since perhaps nothing displays the inherent littleness of an imaginative writer more than the petulance or affected indignation with which he presumes to regard the world of woman. The whole series of Chapman's comedies and tragedies contains, so far as I know, not one woman whose chastity is superior to temptation, whose wit is adaptable to other purposes than those of greedy or amatory intrigue, or whose disposition presents any of those features of sweetness and fidelity which it is the delight of a high-minded poet to dwell upon and to extol, and which most of the Elizabethans and Jacobeans, however base their fancy might take leave to be, never neglected to value.

At the opening of his dramatic career under Elizabeth, Chapman had published some strange and obscure poems which it is not our place to speak of here. But when he ceased to write plays, he turned his attention to poetry again. He dedicated to Prince Henry, in 1609, *The Tears of Peace*, and to the memory of the same "most dear and heroical patron," his *Epicedium* in 1612. *Eugenia*, an elegy on William, Lord Russell, appeared in 1614, and *Andromeda Liberata*, an epithalamium on the scandalous nuptials of Robert Carr and Frances, Lady Essex, in the same year. As late as the summer of 1633 Chapman wrote, but did not conclude, an *Invocation against Ben Jonson*. All these were composed in the heroic couplet. Of these poems *The Tears of Peace* is by far the most valuable, although

Eugenia contains some highly wrought description of natural phenomena.

Here is a rising storm out of the latter poem—

> Heaven's drooping face was dress'd
> In gloomy thunderstocks ; earth, seas, arrayed
> In all presage of storm ; the bitterns played
> And met in flocks ; the herons set clamours gone
> That rattled up air's triple region ;
> The cormorants to dry land did address,
> And cried away all fowls that used the seas ;
> The wanton swallows jerked the standing springs,
> Met in dull lakes, and flew so close, their wings
> Shaved the top waters ; frogs croaked ; the swart crow
> Measured the sea-sands, with pace passing slow,
> And often soused her ominous heat of blood
> Quite over head and shoulders in the flood,
> Still scolding at the rain's so slow access ;
> The trumpet-throated, the Naupliades,
> Their clangours threw about, and summoned up
> All clouds to crown imperious tempest's cup.

In all, as Mr. Swinburne has said, "the allegory is clouded and confounded by all manner of perversities and obscurities, the verse hoarse and stiff, the style dense and convulsive, inaccurate and violent," with occasional lucid intervals of exquisite harmony, which affect the senses strangely in the midst of balderdash so raucous and uncouth.

It is, however, pre-eminently as a translator that Chapman takes high rank among the English poets. In 1598 he had published two small quartos, *Seven Books of the Iliads of Homer* and *The Shield of Achilles*, both dedicated to the Earl of Essex. In 1600 he completed Marlowe's exquisite *Hero and Leander,*

keeping much closer to the text of Musæus. Prince
Henry was among those who read and admired the
Homer fragments, and he commanded Chapman to
complete his translation. Accordingly, in 1609, in folio,
appeared *Homer, Prince of Poets,* a version of the first
twelve books of the *Iliad.* This was identical with the
text of 1598, but with five books added. The entire
Iliad was not published until 1611. In 1612, Chapman
issued the *Penetential Psalms* of Petrarch. He returned,
in spite of Prince Henry's death, to the translation of
Homer, and published the first twelve books of the
Odyssey in 1614, and the remainder of that epic in the
next year. The *Iliad* and *Odyssey* appeared in one
volume in 1616, and Chapman completed his version of
Homer with the *Batrachomyomachia* printed, without
a date, probably in 1622. Meanwhile, Chapman had
been busy with Hesiod, and published a version of the
Georgics, now extremely rare, in 1618; the *Just Reproof
of a Roman Smell-feast,* translated from Juvenal, appeared
in 1629. His violent quarrel with Jonson is, unfortunately, the latest fact which has been preserved
about him ; he died soon after, and was buried in London,
at St. Giles-in-the-Fields, on the 12th of May, 1634.

The noble and famous sonnet written by Keats in
a copy of Chapman's *Homer* is a witness to all time of
the merit of that translation. Busy as Chapman was in
many fields of literature, it is by Homer that he lives
and will continue to live. He threw such an incomparable
fire and gusto into the long, wave-like couplets of his
Iliad, that poet after poet has been borne upon them into
a new world of imagination.

Here is an example from the fifteenth book—

> Then on the ships all Troy,
> Like raw-flesh-nourish'd lions rushed, and knew they did employ
> Their powers to perfect Jove's high will; who still their spirits
>   enflamed,
> And quench'd the Grecians'; one renown'd, the other often sham'd.
> For Hector's glory still he stood, and even went about
> To make him cast the fleet such fire, as never should go out;
> Heard Thetis foul petitión, and wish'd in any wise
> The splendour of the burning ships might satiate his eyes.
> From him yet the repulse was then to be on Troy conferr'd,
> The honour of it given the Greeks; which thinking on, he stirr'd
> With such addition of his spirit, the spirit Hector bore
> To burn the fleet, that of itself was hot enough before.
> But now he far'd like Mars himself, so brandishing his lance
> As, through the deep shades of a wood, a raging fire should glance,
> Held up to all eyes by a hill; about his lips a foam
> Stood as when th' ocean is enrag'd, his eyes were overcomé
> With fervour, and resembled flames, set off by his dark brows
> And from his temples his bright helm abhorrèd lightnings throws.

Chapman "speaks out loud and bold," and the ancient world of Homer, with all its romantic purity and freshness, lies spread at our feet. It has often been noted with amazement that Chapman, whose original poems are perverse and cloudy to the last degree, should have been able so to clarify his style, and so to appreciate the lucidity of his original, as to write a translation of Homer which a boy may read with pleasure. The *Odyssey* of Chapman, which, like the *Hymns*, is in heroic couplet, has never been such a general favourite as the *Iliad*, where the rolling fourteen syllable line carried with it much of the melody and the movement of the Greek hexameter. His success, even here, is irregular and uncertain; sometimes he sinks into platitude or rushes into doggerel; sometimes he is outrageously false to his original and careless of the text. But, on the whole, no later verse-translator of Homer,—and translators have been myriad—has surpassed Chapman, and his *Iliad* remains one of the ornaments of our literature, and one of the principal poetical glories of the Jacobean age.

CHAPTER III.

JOHN DONNE.

AMONG the non-dramatic poets who flourished under James I., incomparably the most singular and influential was the Roman Catholic scholar who became Dean of St. Paul's. John Donne was thirty years of age when Elizabeth died, and no small portion of his most characteristic work must have been written in her reign. But Donne belongs, essentially, to that of her successor. In him the Jacobean spirit, as opposed to the Elizabethan, is paramount. His were the first poems which protested, in their form alike and their tendency, against the pastoral sweetness of the Spenserians. Something new in English literature begins in Donne, something which proceeded, under his potent influence, to colour poetry for nearly a hundred years. The exact mode in which that influence was immediately distributed is unknown to us, or very dimly perceived. To know more about it is one of the great desiderata of literary history. The imitation of Donne's style begins so early, and becomes so general, that several critics have taken for granted that there must have been editions of his writings which have disappeared.

As a matter of fact, with the exception of two exceedingly slight appearances, that of ten sonnets contributed to Davison's *Poetical Rhapsody* in 1602, and of *An Anatomy of the World* in 1611, the poems of Donne are not known to have been printed until 1633, a year or two after his death. Yet the references to them in documents of twenty years earlier are frequent, and that they were widely distributed is certain. This was doubtless done by means of more or less complete transcripts, several of which have come down to our own day. These transcripts must have been passed from hand to hand at court, at the universities, in cultured country houses, and almost every poet of the Jacobean age must have been more or less familiar with their tenor. The style of Donne, like a very odd perfume, was found to cling to every one who touched it, and we observe the remarkable phenomenon of poems which had not passed through a printer's hands exercising the influence of a body of accepted classical work. In estimating the poetry of the Jacobean age, therefore, there is no writer who demands more careful study than this enigmatical and subterranean master, this veiled Isis whose utterances outweighed the oracles of all the visible gods.

For the secrecy with which the poems of Donne were produced no adequate reason is forthcoming. His conduct in other respects, though somewhat haughty, was neither cloistered nor mysterious. He was profuse in the publication of his prose writings, and denied his verse alone to his admirers. That the tenor of it clashed with his profession as a Churchman has been put forward as a reason, but it is not a very good one. Donne was not squeamish in his sermons, nor afraid of misconception in his *Pseudo-Martyr*. If he had had scruples of conscience about his secular poems he might have destroyed them, as George Herbert did his. It is idle to speculate on the cause of Donne's peculiar conduct. It suffices to record that having produced a quantity of poetry of extraordinary value, and intimately welcome to his generation, he would neither publish nor destroy it, but permitted, and perhaps preferred, that it should circulate among his most intelligent contemporaries in such a way as to excite the maximum of curiosity and mystery.

John Donne was born in the city of London in 1573; his father was a Welshman, his mother descended from the family of Sir Thomas More. At an early age he showed precocious talents, and was educated with care at Oxford first, and then possibly at Cambridge. Before he was fourteen he had won the title of the Pico della Mirandola of his age. His father died when he was a child, and left him in the charge of a mother who was a Roman Catholic herself, and greatly desired to see her son converted. For a long time the young man hung undecided, between the Churches of Rome and England. While in this uncertain condition of mind, of which Izaak Walton has preserved a record, Donne wrote, or began to write, his *Satires*, which are understood to belong to the years 1593 and 1594. He threw in his lot with the Earl of Essex, and, in a brief heat of soldier-ship, took part in the expedition against Cadiz, and in the Island Voyage. From the Azores he passed into

Italy, and thence into Spain, making himself familiar
with contemporary thought in those countries. Returning to England, he became secretary to the Lord
Chancellor, and eventually fell in love with a young
lady of quality who was Lady Elsemore's niece. This
attachment lost for Donne the favour of his patron, but
after romantic difficulties the marriage was performed
in 1600, although the poet was immediately thrown into
prison.

He was soon released, but he found it impossible to
regain his situation. His wife and he, however, were
invited by their kinsman, Francis Wolley, to take up
their abode at his country-seat of Pyrford, which they
did. The next few years were spent in this retirement,
absorbed in intellectual work of all kinds, and were in all
probability those in which the radiating heat of Donne's
genius first began to make itself felt. On the death of
Wolley, the Donnes retired to a house in Mitcham in 1606,
while the poet took lodgings in London for his more
frequent communication with those who, from all parts
of Europe, now began to gather to listen to his conversation. In 1610, James I., who "had formerly both
known and put a value upon his company, and had also
given him some hopes of a state employment, being
always much pleased when Mr. Donne attended him,"
suddenly adjured him to enter the ministry. Donne
declined to do so on the spot, but from that time forth
he gave his special attention to "an incessant study of
textual divinity," and in 1615, at the age of forty-two,
he took holy orders. He quickly rose to be Dean of
St. Paul's, a post which he held for nearly nine years,

dying on the 31st of March, 1631, of a consumption. At
the time of his death he was, beyond question, the most
admired preacher in England. This brief sketch of the
external circumstances of Donne's life may be sufficient
for our purpose, but gives no idea of the mysterious dis-
crepancies which existed in his character, of the singular
constitution of his mind, or of his fiery eccentricity.

With the trifling exceptions which have been mentioned
above, the poems of Donne were not published until
after his death. The first edition, the quarto of 1633,
is very inaccurate and ill-arranged; the octavos of 1635
and 1639 are much fuller and more exact. Donne,
however, still lacks a competent editor. We have no
direct knowledge of the poet's own wish as to the
arrangement of his poems, nor any safe conjecture as to
the date of more than a few pieces. The best lyrics,
however, appear to belong to the first decade of James
I.'s reign, if they are not even of earlier composition.
There seems to be no doubt that the *Satires*, an imperfect
manuscript of which bears the date 1593, are wholly
Elizabethan. These are seven in number, and belong to
the same general category as those of Hall, Lodge, and
Guilpin. Neither in date nor in style do they belong
to the period treated of in this volume, and it is therefore
not necessary to dwell on them at great length here.
They are brilliant and picturesque beyond any of their
particular compeers, even beyond the best of Hall's
satires. But they have the terrible faults which marked
all our Elizabethan satirists, a crabbed violence alike of
manner and matter, a fierce voluble conventionality,
a tortured and often absolutely licentious and erroneous

conception of the use of language. The fourth is, doubtless, the best written, and may be taken as the best essay in this class of poetry existing in English literature before the middle-life of Dryden ; its attraction for Pope is well known.

"The Progress of the Soul," as named by its author "Poema Satyricon," takes its natural place after the satires, but is conjectured to have been written not earlier than 1610. De Quincey, with unwonted warmth, declared that "massy diamonds compose the very substance of this poem, thoughts and descriptions which have the fervent and gloomy sublimity of Ezekiel or Æschylus." It is written in a variant of the Spenserian stanza, and is a hyperbolical history of the development of the human soul, extended to more than five hundred lines, and not ended, but abruptly closed. It is one of the most difficult of Donne's writings, and started a kind of psychological poetry of which, as the century progressed, many more examples were seen, none, perhaps, of a wholly felicitous character. It has the poet's characteristics, however, to the full. The verse marches with a virile tread, the epithets are daring, the thoughts always curious and occasionally sublime, the imagination odd and scholastic, with recurring gleams of passion.

Here is a fragment of this strange production—

> Into an embryon fish our soul is thrown,
> And in due time thrown out again, and grown
> To such vastness, as if, unmanacled
> From Greece, Morea were, and that, by some
> Earthquake unrooted, loose Morea swum,
> Or seas from Afric's body had severèd

And torn the hopeful promontory's head ;
This fish would seem these, and, when all hopes fail,
A great ship overset, or without sail
   Hulling, might (when this was a whelp) be like this whale.

At every stroke his brazen fins do take
More circles in the broken sea they make
Then cannons' voices, when the air they tear ;
His ribs are pillars, and his high-arch'd roof,
Of bark that blunts best steel, is thunder-proof ;
Swim in him, swallow'd dolphins, without fear,
And feel no sides, as if his vast womb were
Some inland sea, and ever as he went
He spouted rivers up, as if he meant
   To join our seas with seas above the firmament.
   *   *   *   *   *
Now drinks he up seas, and he eats up flocks ;
He jostles islands and he shakes firm rocks ;
Now in a roomful house this soul doth float,
And like a prince she sends her faculties
To all her limbs, distant as provinces.
The Sun hath twenty times both crab and goat
Parchèd, since first launch'd forth this living boat ;
'Tis greatest now and to destruction
Nearest ; there's no pause at perfection,
   Greatness a period hath, but hath no station.

Far less extraordinary are the Epistles, which form a
large section of Donne's poetical works. All through
life he was wont to address letters, chiefly in the heroic
couplet, to the most intimate of his friends. These
epistles are conceived in a lighter vein than his other
writings, and have less of his characteristic vehemence.
The earliest, however, " The Storm," which he addressed
from the Azores, possesses his Elizabethan mannerism ;
it is crudely picturesque and licentious, essentially un-
poetical. " The Calm," which is the parallel piece, is

far better, and partly deserves Ben Jonson's high commendation of it to Drummond. The epistle to Sir Henry Goodyer is noticeable for the dignified and stately manner in which the four-line stanza, afterwards adopted by Gray for his *Elegy*, is employed ; this poem is exceedingly like the early pieces written by Dryden some fifty years later. The school of the Restoration is plainly foreshadowed in it.

Many of these epistles are stuffed hard with thoughts, but poetry is rarely to be found in them ; the style is not lucid, the construction is desperately parenthetical. It is not often that the weary reader is rewarded by such a polished piece of versification as is presented by this passage about love in the " Letter to the Countess of Huntingdon."

> It is not love that sueth, or doth contend ;
> Love either conquers, or but meets a friend.
> Man's better part consists of purer fire,
> And finds itself allowed, ere it desire.
> Love is wise here, keeps home, gives reason sway,
> And journeys not till it find summer-way.
> A weather-beaten lover, but once known,
> Is sport for every girl to practise on.
> Who strives, through woman's scorns, woman to know,
> Is lost, and seeks his shadow to outgo ;
> It must be sickness, after one disdain,
> Though he be called aloud, to look again ;
> Let others sin and grieve ; one cunning slight
> Shall freeze my love to crystal in a night.
> I can love first, and, if I win, love still,
> And cannot be removed, unless she will ;
> It is her fault if I unsure remain ;
> She only can untie, I bind again ;
> The honesties of love with ease I do,
> But am no porter for a tedious woe.

Most of these epistles are New Year's greetings, and
many are addressed to the noble and devout ladies
with whom he held spiritual converse in advancing years.
The poet superbly aggrandizes the moral qualities of
these women, paying to their souls the court that
younger and flightier cavaliers reserved for the physical
beauty of their daughters.

The Epithalamia of Donne form that section of his
work in which, alone, he seems to follow in due succession after Spenser. These marriage-songs are elegant and
glowing, though not without the harshness which Donne
could not for any length of time forego. That composed
for the wedding of Frederick Count Palatine and the Lady
Elizabeth, in 1613, is perhaps the most popular of all
Donne's writings, and opens with a delicious vivacity.

> Hail, Bishop Valentine, whose day this is !
>   All the air is thy diocese,
>   And all the chirping choristers
> And other birds are thy parishioners ;
>   Thou marryest every year
> The lyric lark and the grave whispering dove,
> The sparrow that neglects his life for love,
> The household bird with the red stomacher ;
> Thou mak'st the blackbird speed as soon
> As doth the goldfinch or the halcyon ;
> The husband cock looks out, and straight is sped,
> And meets his wife, which brings her feather-bed.
> This day more cheerfully than ever shine,—
> This day, which might enflame thyself, old Valentine.

The ode within the rather stiff setting of the Allo-
phanes and Idios eclogue is scarcely less felicitous.

The miscellaneous secular poems of Donne are
generically classed under the heading of " Elegies." We

have here some of the most extraordinary aberrations
of fancy, some of the wildest contrasts of character
and style, to be observed in literature. They are
mainly Ovidian or Tibullan studies of the progress
of the passion of love, written by one who proclaims
himself an ardent, but no longer an illusioned lover,—
hot, still, but violent and scandalous. The youth of the
author is disclosed in them, but it is not the callous
youth of first inexperience. He is already a past
master in the subtle sophistry of love, and knows by
rote " the mystic language of the eye and hand." Weary
with the beauty of spring and summer, he has learned
to find fascination in an autumnal face. The voluptuous
character of these elegies has scandalized successive
critics. Several of them, to be plain, were indeed too
outspoken for the poet's own, or for any decent age.
Throughout it is seldom so much what the unbridled
lover says, as his utter intemperance in saying it, that
surprises, especially in one who, by the time the poems
were given to the public, had come to be regarded as
the holiest of men. Even saints, however, were coarse
in the age of James, and the most beautiful of all Donne's
elegies, the exquisite " Refusal to allow his Young Wife
to accompany him abroad as a Page," which belongs to
his mature life and treats of a very creditable passion, is
marred by almost inconceivable offences against good
taste.

Another section of Donne's poems is composed of
funeral elegies or requiems, in which he allowed the
sombre part of his fancy to run riot. In these curious
entombments we read nothing that seems personal or

pathetic, but much about "the magnetic force" of the
deceased, her spiritual anatomy, and her soul's "meri-
dians and parallels." Amid these pedantries, we light
now and then upon extraordinary bursts of poetic obser-
vation, as when the eminence of the spirit of Mistress
Drury reminds the poet of a vision, seen years before in
sailing past the Canaries, and he cries out—

> Doth not a Teneriffe or higher hill,
> Rise so high like a rock, that one might think
> The floating moon would shipwreck there, and sink,

or as when one of his trances comes upon him, and he
sighs—

> when thou know'st this,
> Thou know'st how wan a ghost this our world is.

These lovely sudden bursts of pure poetry are more
frequent in the "Funeral Elegies" than in any section of
Donne's poetry which we have mentioned, and approach
those, to be presently noted, in the Lyrics. The spirit of
this strange writer loved to dwell on the majestic and
gorgeous aspects of death, to wave his torch within the
charnel-house and to show that its walls are set with
jewels.

This may be taken as an example of his obscure
mortuary imagination—

> As men of China, after an age's stay,
> Do take up porcelain where they buried clay,
> So at this grave, her limbeck (which refines
> The diamonds, rubies, sapphires, pearls and mines
> Of which this flesh was), her soul shall inspire
> Flesh of such stuff, as God, when his last fire
> Annuls this world, to recompense it, shall
> Make and name them the elixir of this All.

They say, the sea, when it gains, loseth too,
If carnal Death (the younger brother) do
Usurp the body ; our soul, which subject is
To the elder Death, by sin, is freed by this ;
They perish both, when they attempt the just,
For graves our trophies are, and both death's dust.

The presence of the emblems of mortality rouses
Donne to an unusual intellectual ecstasy. The latest
of these elegies is dated 1625, and shows that the poet
retained his art in this kind of writing to the very
close of his career, adding polish to his style, without any
perceptible falling off in power.

A large number of " Holy Sonnets," which Izaak
Walton thought had perished, were published in 1669,
and several remain still unprinted. They are more
properly quatorzains than sonnets, more correct in form
than the usual English sonnet of the age—for the octett
is properly arranged and rhymed—but closing in the
sestett with a couplet. These sonnets are very interesting
from the light they throw on Donne's prolonged sympathy
with the Roman Church, over which his biographers
have been wont to slur. All these " Holy Sonnets " probably belong to 1617, or the period immediately following the death of Donne's wife. In the light of certain
examples in the possession of the present writer, which
have not yet appeared in print, they seem to confirm
Walton's remark that though Donne inquired early in
life into the differences between Protestantism and
Catholicism, yet that he lived until the death of his
wife without religion.

A pathetic sonnet from the Westmoreland manuscript,

here printed for the first time, shows the effect of that
bereavement upon him—

> Since she whom I loved hath paid her last debt
>   To Nature, and to hers and my good is dead,
>   And her soul early into heaven vanished.—
> Wholly on heavenly things my mind is set.
> Here the admiring her my mind did whet
>   To seek thee, God ; so streams do show their head,
>   But tho' I have found thee, and thou my thirst hast fed,
> A holy thirsty dropsy melts me yet.
> But why should I beg more love, when as thou
>   Does woo my soul for hers, off'ring all thine :
> And dost not only fear lest I allow
>   My love to Saints and Angels, things divine,
> But in thy tender jealousy dost doubt
> Lest this World, Flesh, yea Devil put thee out ?

The sonnet on the Blessed Virgin Mary, however,
has probably been attributed to Donne by error; the
more likely name of Constable has been suggested as
that of its author.

In his other divine poems, also, the Roman element is
often very strong, and the theology of a cast which is far
removed from that of Puritanism. In the very curious
piece called " The Cross," he seems to confess to the use
of a material crucifix, and in " A Litany " he distinctly
recommends prayer to the Virgin Mary,

> " That she-cherubim which unlocked Paradise."

All these are matters which must be left to the future
biographers of Donne, but which are worthy of their
closest attention in developing the intricate anomalies
of his character.

We have now, by a process of exhaustion, arrived at

what is the most interesting of the sections of Donne's poetry, his amatory lyrics. These are about seventy in number, and so far as the scanty evidence can be depended upon, belong to various periods from his twentieth to his thirty-fifth year. The series, as we now hold it, begins with the gross and offensive piece of extravagance called, "The Flea," but is followed by "The Good-Morrow," which strikes a very different note. As a rule, these poems are extremely personal, confidential, and vivid; the stamp of life is on them. None the less, while confessing with extraordinary frankness and clearness the passion of the writer, they are so reserved in detail, so immersed and engulphed in secrecy, that no definite conjecture can be hazarded as to the person, or persons, or the class of persons, to whom they were addressed. One or two were evidently inspired by Donne's wife, others most emphatically were not, and in their lawless, though not gross, sensuality, remind us of the still more outspoken "Elegies." In spite of the alembicated verbiage, the tortuousness and artificiality of the thought, sincerity burns in every stanza, and the most exquisite images lie side by side with monstrous conceits and ugly pedantries.

A peculiarity of the lyrics is that scarcely two of the seventy are written in the same verse-form. Donne evidently laid himself out to invent elaborate and far-fetched metres. He was imitated in this down to the Restoration, when all metrical effects tended to merge in the heroic couplet. But of the innumerable form-inventions of Donne and of his disciples scarcely one has been adopted into the language, although more than one, by their elegance and melody, deserve to be resumed.

This exemplifies one of the prettiest of his stanza-forms—

> Íf thou be'st born to strange sights,
>   Things invisible to see,
> Ride ten thousand days and nights,
>   Till age snow white hairs on thee ;
> Thou, when thou return'st, wilt tell me
> All strange wonders that befell thee,
>   And swear
>   Nowhere
> Lives a woman true and fair.
>
> If thou find'st one, let me know ;
>   Such a pilgrimage were sweet.
> Yet do not,—I would not go
>   Though at next door we might meet,
> Though she were true when you met her,
> And last till you write your letter,
>   Yet she
>   Will be
> False, ere I come, with two or three.

It now remains to examine this body of poetry in general terms, and, first of all, it is necessary to make some remarks with regard to Donne's whole system of prosody. The terms " irregular," " unintelligible," and " viciously rugged," are commonly used in describing it, and it seems even to be supposed by some critics that Donne did not know how to scan. This last supposition may be rejected at once ; what there was to know about poetry was known to Donne. But it seems certain that he intentionally introduced a revolution into English versification. It was doubtless as a rebellion against the smooth and somewhat nerveless iambic flow of Spenser and the earliest contemporaries of Shakespeare, that Donne invented his violent mode of breaking up the line into quick and slow beats. The best critic of his own generation, Ben Jonson, hated the innovation, and told Drummond "that Donne, for not keeping of accent, deserved hanging." It is difficult to stem a current of censure which has set without intermission since the very days of Donne itself, but I may be permitted to point out what I imagine was the poet's own view of the matter.

He found, as I have said, the verse of his youth, say of 1590, exceedingly mellifluous, sinuous, and inclining to flaccidity. A five-syllabled iambic line of Spenser or of Daniel trots along with the gentlest amble of inevitable shorts and longs. It seems to have vexed the ear of Donne by its tendency to feebleness, and it doubtless appeared to him that the very gifted writers who immediately preceded him had carried the softness of it as far as it would go. He desired new and more varied effects. To see what he aimed at doing, we have, I believe, to turn to what has been attempted in our own time, by Mr. Robert Bridges, in some of his early experiments, and by the Symbolists in France. The iambic rhymed line of Donne has audacities such as are permitted to his blank verse by Milton, and although the felicities are rare in the older poet, instead of being almost incessant, as in the later, Donne at his best is not less melodious than Milton. When he writes—

Blasted with sighs and surrounded with tears,

we must not dismiss this as not being iambic verse at
all, nor,—much less,—attempt to read it—

> Blastéd with síghs, and súrroundéd with teárs,

but recognize in it the poet's attempt to identify the
beat of his verse with his bewildered and dejected condition, reading it somewhat in this notation :—

> Blasted | with sighs ‖ and surrounded | with tears.

The violence of Donne's transposition of accent is
most curiously to be observed in his earliest satires, and
in some of his later poems is almost entirely absent.
Doubtless his theory became modified with advancing
years. No poet is more difficult to read aloud. Such
a passage as the following may excusably defy a
novice :—

> No token of worth but Queen's man and fine
> Living barrels of beef and flagons of wine.
> I shook like a spied spy.   Preachers which are
> Seas of wit and arts, you can then dare
> Drown the sins of this place, for, for me,
> Which am but a scant brook, it enough shall be
> To wash the stains away.

But treat the five-foot verse not as a fixed and unalter-
able sequence of cadences, but as a norm around which
a musician weaves his variations, and the riddle is soon
read—

> No token | of worth | but Queen's | man | and fine
> Living | barrels of | beef and | flagons of | wine.
> I shook | like a spied | spy. | Preachers | which are
> Seas | of wit | and arts, | you can then | dare
> Drown | the sins | of this place, | for, | for me,
> Which am | but a scant | brook, | it enough | shall be
> To wash | the stains | away.

The poetry of Donne possesses in no small degree that "unusual and indefinable witchery" which Dr. Jessopp has noted as characteristic of the man himself. But our enjoyment of it is marred by the violence of the writer, by his want of what seems to us to be good taste, and by a quality which has been overlooked by those who have written about him, but which seems to provide the key to the mystery of his position. Donne was, I would venture to suggest, by far the most modern and contemporaneous of the writers of his time. He rejected all the classical tags and imagery of the Elizabethans, he borrowed nothing from French or Italian tradition. He arrived at an excess of actuality in style, and it was because he struck them as so novel and so completely in touch with his own age that his immediate coevals were so much fascinated with him. His poems are full of images taken from the life and habits of the time. Where earlier poets had summoned the myths of Greece to adorn their verse, Donne weaves in, instead, the false zoology, the crude physics and philosophy, of his own fermenting epoch. The poem called "Love's Exchange," is worthy of careful examination in this respect. Each stanza is crowded with conceits, each one of which is taken from the practical or professional life of the moment in which the poet wrote. This extreme modernness, however, is one potent source of our lack of sympathy with the poetry so inspired. In the long run, it is the broader suggestion, the wider if more conventional range of classic imagery, which may hope to hold without fatigue the interest of successive generations.

For us the charm of Donne continues to rest in his
occasional felicities, his bursts of melodious passion.
If his song were not so tantalizingly fragmentary, we
should call him the unquestioned nightingale of the
Jacobean choir. No other poet of that time, few poets
of any time, have equalled the concentrated passion,
the delicate, long-drawn musical effects, the bold and
ecstatic rapture of Donne at his best. In such a poem
as " The Dream," he realizes the very paroxysm of
amatory song. In his own generation, no one approached
the purity of his cascades of ringing monosyllables, his

> For God's sake, hold your tongue and let me love,

or,

> I long to talk with some old lover's ghost,
> Who died before the God of Love was born,

or,

> Oh more than moon,
> Draw not thy seas to drown me in thy sphere.

or,

> A bracelet of bright hair about the bone.

In these and similar passages, of which a not very
slender florilegium might be gathered from his voluminous
productions, Donne reminds us that Ben Jonson esteemed
him " the first poet in the world in some things." But
this quality of passionate music is not the only one
discernible, nor often to be discerned. The more
obvious characteristic was summed up by Coleridge in
a droll quatrain—

> With Donne, whose Muse on dromedary trots,
> Wreathe iron pokers into true-love-knots ;
> Rhyme's sturdy cripple, Fancy's maze and clue,
> Wit's forge and fire-blast, Meaning's press and screw.

In the use of these ingenuities, which it was once the fashion to call "metaphysical," Donne shows an amazing pertinacity. He is never daunted by the feeling that his wit is exercised "on subjects where we have no right to expect it," and where it is impossible for us to relish it. He pushes on with relentless logic,—sometimes, indeed, past chains of images that are lovely and appropriate ; but, oftener, through briars and lianas that rend his garments and trip up his feet. He is not affected by the ruggedness of his road, nor by our unwillingness to follow him. He stumbles doggedly on until he has reached his singular goal. In all this intellectual obstinacy he has a certain kinship to Browning, but his obscurity is more dense. It is to be hoped that the contemporary maligned him who reported Donne to have written one of his elegies in an intentional obscureness, but that he delighted in putting his readers out of their depth can scarcely be doubted. It is against this lurid background, which in itself and unrelieved would possess a very slight attraction to modern readers, that the electrical flashes of Donne's lyrical intuition make their appearance, almost blinding us by their brilliancy, and fading into the dark tissue of conceits before we have time to appreciate them.

The prominence here given to Donne will be challenged by no one who considers what his influence was on the poetical taste of the time. It is true that among his immediate contemporaries the following of Spenser did not absolutely cease at once. But if a study on the poets of Charles I. were to succeed the present volume, the name of Donne would have to be constantly prominent. On almost everything non-dramatic published in the succeeding generation, from Crashaw to Davenant, from Carew to Cowley, the stamp of Donne is set. Dryden owed not a little to him, although, as time went on, he purged himself more and more fully of the taint of metaphysical conceit. So late as 1692, in the preface to *Eleanora*, Dryden still held up Donne as "the greatest wit, though not the best poet of our nation." His poems were among the few non-dramatic works of the Jacobean period which continued to be read and reprinted in the age of Anne, and Pope both borrowed from and imitated Donne.

So far as we trace this far-sweeping influence exercised on the poets of a hundred years, we have difficulty in applauding its effects. The empassioned sincerity, the intuitions, the clarion note of Donne were individual to himself and could not be transmitted. It was far otherwise with the jargon of "metaphysical" wit, the trick of strained and inappropriate imagery. These could be adopted by almost any clever person, and were, in fact, employed with fluent effect by people in whom the poetical quality was of the slightest. Writers like Mildmay Fane, Earl of Westmoreland, or like Owen Feltham (in his verse), show what it was that Donne's seed produced when it fell upon stony ground.

CHAPTER IV.

BEAUMONT AND FLETCHER.

THERE is no body of poetical work which displays so characteristically—we may not add, perhaps, so favourably—the qualities of the Jacobean age as the mass of plays united under the names of Beaumont and Fletcher. These celebrated friends, who supply the most illustrious example of the art of literary partnership now extant, would probably be as little known to us as several of their scarcely less-gifted contemporaries, if they had not so exactly gratified the taste of their time, and of the generation which succeeded theirs, as to induce the players to preserve and revise their writings. Only ten of their plays were printed during their lives, but the folio of 1647 saved forty-two others from a destruction which may have been imminent.

As the century proceeded, the writings of these friends advanced in popularity far beyond that of Shakespeare's or even of Ben Jenson's, and when the Restoration thought of the classic English drama, it thought principally of Beaumont and Fletcher. Dryden expressed the common opinion when he said that they reproduced the easy conversation of gentlefolks more ably than Shakespeare, and

acquiesced in the common taste when he recorded that
in his day "two of theirs were acted through the year,
for one of Shakespeare's or Jonson's." Beaumont and
Fletcher preserved their vogue until the classic reaction
was completed, and then their romantic plots and easy
verse went suddenly out of fashion. Towards the end
of the eighteenth century their fame revived, but it has
never again risen to its first commanding height. Yet the
richness and abundance of these dramatists, their very
high level of merit, and their perfect sympathy with the
age in which they flourished, will always save them from
critical neglect. To praise them unreservedly is no
longer possible; but no one who loves poetry can fail to
read them with delight.

Of the famous Heavenly Twins of Parnassus, John
Fletcher was the elder. He was born in December, 1579,
at Rye, of which parish his father, Richard Fletcher,
was then incumbent. Dr. Fletcher became successively
Bishop of Bristol, of Worcester, and of London, dying
when his son was seventeen, and an inmate of Bene't
College, Cambridge. Fletcher's career is entirely
obscure to us, until he began to be a dramatist, in his
thirtieth year; but it is probable that, though not rich, he
never found himself so pinched by poverty as the
majority of his dramatic colleagues were. Francis
Beaumont was even more certainly in easy circumstances.
He was born, the third son of the squire of Grace-Dieu
in Leicestershire, towards the close of 1584. He was
admitted to Broadgates Hall, Oxford, in 1597, and
proceeded to the Inner Temple three years later. He
was probably the author of *Salmacis and Hermaphrodite,*

1602, a luscious paraphrase of a story of Ovid told in heroic verse, a juvenile performance, but one of high poetic promise.   Early in the century Beaumont became a prominent figure among the wits, and was little more than of age when Ben Jonson addressed him—

> How do I love thee, Beaumont,·and thy Muse,

in answer to the complimentary "religion" of a neatly turned copy of verses on *Volpone*.   Fletcher wrote on the same occasion, and their names are thus for the first time connected.   The famous meetings at the Mermaid may have begun soon after 1606, when Beaumont composed his *Letter to Ben Jonson*, "written before he and Master Fletcher came to London."   He says in the course of this admirable epistle :—

> What things have we seen
> Done at the Mermaid ; heard words that have been
> So nimble and so full of subtle flame,
> As if that every one from whence they came,
> Had meant to put his whole wit in a jest,
> And had resolved to live a fool the rest
> Of his dull life.

From this same poem, in which he speaks of "scenes" which are not yet perfect, we see that he was already a dramatist.   The first appearance he is known to have made was in the comedy of *The Woman-Hater*, written and anonymously printed in 1607.   There is little doubt that this was the unaided work of Beaumont.   It bears manifest signs of a young hand, and is a crude miscellany of prose patched with soft passages of romantic blank verse.   *The Woman-Hater* is interesting as manifestly composed under the influence of Shakespeare.   The

central figure is a hungry courtier, Lazarillo, who studies
greediness as a fine art, and indulges in exquisite
rhapsodies of longing for the head of an "umbrano,"
which fishy delicacy evades him to the last. The fair
adventuress Oriana is a species of Beatrice, and Gondarino
an unseemly and extravagant Benedick. The scene is
laid at Milan; the verse is primitive, and the knowledge
of stage-craft as yet rudimentary. None the less, the
germ of the whole Beaumont-and-Fletcher drama is to
be traced in this lax and luxurious mixture of poetry and
farce.

In 1608 Fletcher is believed to have made his first
essay in authorship with the pastoral tragi-comedy of
The Faithful Shepherdess, which is admitted to be, from
the purely poetical point of view, one of the best, if not
the very best thing of its kind in English. There is no
reason to suppose that at this point he had begun to
combine with Beaumont, and this poem has all the
air of being Fletcher's unaided composition, in spite of
a phrase of Jonson's to Drummond. *The Faithful
Shepherdess* was an attempt to introduce into English
literature the art of Tasso and Guarini. It is an artificial
and exotic piece, of little dramatic propriety, and even
when it was originally produced, it made the audience
angry by its substitution of *renaissance* fancies for
"Whitsun-ales, cream, wassail and morris-dances." It
is an excursion into the very fairyland of imagination;
but, unfortunately, Fletcher carries with him the grossness
and the moral perversity which were his most unfortunate
characteristics, and his wanton shepherdesses are scan-
dalously indifferent to decorum. On the other hand, no

work of the period abounds with finer lyrical beauties, truer touches of sympathy with nature, or more artfully artless turns of exquisite language.

Here are two fragments of the Satyr's speeches—

> See, the day begins to break,
> And the light shoots like a streak
> Of subtle fire ; the wind blows cold,
> As the morning doth unfold ;
> Now the birds begin to rouse,
> And the squirrel from the boughs
> Leaps to get him nuts and fruit ;
> The early lark, that erst was mute,
> Carols to the rising day
> Many a note and many a lay.

> Thou divinest, fairest, brightest,
> Thou most powerful Maid, and whitest,
> Thou most virtuous and most blessèd,
> Eyes of stars, and golden-tressèd
> Like Apollo, tell me, Sweetest,
> What new service now is meetest
> For the Satyr?   Shall I stray
> In the middle air, and stay
> The sailing rack, or nimbly take
> Hold by the moon, and gently make
> Suit to the pale queen of night
> For a beam to give them light?
> Shall I dive into the sea,
> And bring the coral, making way
> Through the rising waves that fall
> In snowy fleeces?   Dearest, shall
> I catch the wanton fawns, or flies
> Whose woven wings the summer dyes
> Of many colours?   Get thee fruit?
> Or steal from heaven old Orpheus' lute?
> All these I'll venture for, and more,
> To do her service all these woods adore.

The famous partnership of Beaumont and Fletcher began about 1608, and lasted until 1611. During this brief period they wrote ten or eleven of the plays which still exist, and without doubt not a few of their productions are lost. In 1608 * they brought out on the stage *Four Plays in One*, *Love's Cure*, and probably *A King and No King*. In 1609 *The Scornful Lady ;* in 1610 *The Knight of the Burning Pestle*, *The Coxcomb*, *Cupid's Revenge* and *Philaster ;* in 1611 *The Two Noble Kinsmen*, in which Shakespeare may have collaborated, *The Maid's Tragedy*, and perhaps *Love's Pilgrimage*. In 1611 Beaumont, who seems to have always shrunk from the rough publicity of the stage, made up his mind to retire from play-writing ; he had never allowed his name to appear on a title-page. He probably married Ursula Isley at this time, and withdrew to the country. Perhaps his health began to fail ; at all events, on the 6th of March, 1616, at the early age of thirty-one, he died, and was buried, three days later, in Westminster Abbey.

It is in the plays which have just been mentioned that the peculiar qualities of the two playwrights are seen to the best advantage. In later years, whether alone, or in collaboration with others, Fletcher produced many very fine works, but they scarcely have the charm of those which he wrote with Beaumont. When the posthumous editor of 1647 came to arrange the dramas, he placed *The Maid's Tragedy* at the head, *Philaster* next to it, and *A King or No King* third. In these three plays, and in *The Knight of the Burning Pestle*, too, the hand

---

* The conjectural arrangement so ingeniously worked out by Mr. Fleay is here in the main adopted.

of Beaumont appears to be paramount. There is, at least, very marked, a certain element which does not reappear after the retirement of Beaumont, and which may safely be attributed to that writer.

The seventeenth century admired *The Maid's Tragedy* to excess, and it is true that it is full of poetry which it would be hardly possible to overpraise, a poetry which is more delicate, more spontaneous than the declamatory genius of Fletcher could produce unaided.

Here is part of a speech by Aspatia in the second act—

> Then, my good girls, be more than women, wise,—
> At least, be more than I was, and be sure
> You credit anything the light gives light to,
> Before a man ; rather believe the sea
> Weeps for the ruin'd merchant when he roars ;
> Rather the wind courts but the pregnant sails
> When the strong cordage cracks ; rather the sun
> Comes but to kiss the fruit in wealthy autumn,
> When all falls blasted ; if you needs must love,
> Forc'd by ill fate, take to your maiden bosoms
> Two dead-cold aspics, and of them make lovers ;
> They cannot flatter, nor forswear ; one kiss
> Makes a long peace for all ;—but Man,
> Oh ! that beast, Man ! Come ! let's be sad, my girls !

The plot of *The Maid's Tragedy*, the only play of Beaumont and Fletcher's which has been revived on the modern stage, is gross, painful, and improbable. Yet there is tragic interest in the distressing relation of Evadne and Amintor; while in the fifth act, where Evadne kills the king, a certain moral altitude of horror, unusual with these poets, is distinctly reached. In almost every way, for good and ill, *The Maid's Tragedy* is a characteristic specimen of their theatre.

Modern taste prefers *Philaster*, in many ways an
enchanting performance.   The beauty of the imagery
and the melody of the language here become something
veritably astonishing.   Nothing in Jacobean poetry
outside Shakespeare is more charming than the sweet
companionship, in the second act, of Philaster and the
boy-maiden, Bellario-Eufrasia.

It is thus that Philaster describes Bellario —

> I have a boy
> Sent by the gods, I hope to this intent,
> Not yet seen in the court ; hunting the buck,
> I found him sitting by a fountain-side,
> Of which he borrowed some to quench his thirst,
> And paid the nymph again as much in tears ;
> A garland lay him by, made by himself
> Of many several flowers, bred in the bay,
> Stuck in that mystic order, that the rareness
> Delighted me ; but ever when he turned
> His tender eyes upon 'em, he would weep,
> As if he meant to make 'em grow again.
> Seeing such pretty helpless innocence
> Dwell in his face, I asked him all his story :
> He told me that his parents gentle died,
> Leaving him to the mercy of the fields,
> Which gave him roots ; and of the crystal springs,
> Which did not stop their courses ; and the sun,
> Which still, he thank'd him, yielded him his light ;
> Then he took up his garland and did show
> What every flower, as country people hold,
> Did signify ; and how all, order'd thus,
> Express'd his grief ; and to my thoughts did read
> The prettiest lecture of his country art
> That could be wished ; so that methought I could
> Have studied it.   I gladly entertained him,
> Who was more glad to follow, and have got
> The trustiest, lovingest, and the gentlest boy
> That ever master kept.

Bellario's final speech to the king sums up the essence of the play, and explains the prettiest of those rather awkward disguises of boys as girls and girls as boys, in which Sidney and Shakespeare had indulged, but which Beaumont and Fletcher observed in a positive extravagance. Stronger than either of these graceful romances, is the tragi-comedy of *A King and No King*, which sacrifices force less to sweetness than is usual with its authors, and proceeds with great spirit. Arbaces, a finely designed character, moves the accomplished type of a vaunting egotist, the man who is unshaken in the belief in himself. Magnanimous as well as braggart, there is a life-like variety in Arbaces more attractive than the too-Jonsonian figure of Bessus, whose almost professional cowardice is so incessant as to grow tiresome.

Other plays of this first and greatest period which demand a special word are *The Knight of the Burning Pestle*, with its extremely early proof of the popularity of Cervantes; *Four Plays in One*, two by Beaumont and two by Fletcher, which seems to represent their first efforts at combined authorship; *Love's Cure*, a rattling, vigorous comedy of Seville manners, in which Lucio, a lad brought up as a girl, is contrasted with Clara, the martial maid, who dreams herself a man—Love curing them both, and bringing both back to nature; the sparkling English comedy of *The Scornful Lady*, with its domestic scenes; and *The Two Noble Kinsmen*, a stirring but ill-constructed dramatization of Chaucer, to which the shadow of the name of Shakespeare, and a certain indisputable strength in the first act, have directed a somewhat exaggerated amount of attention.

The song with which it opens can scarcely but be by
Shakespeare himself.

> Roses, their sharp spines being gone,
> Not royal in their smells alone,
>   But in their hue,
> Maiden pinks, of odour faint,
> Daisies smell-less, yet most quaint,
>   And sweet thyme true ;
>
> Primrose, first-born child of Ver,
> Many springtime's harbinger,
>   With her bells dim ;
> Oxlips in their cradles growing ;
> Marigolds on death-beds blowing ;
>   Lark-heels trim ;
>
> All dear Nature's children sweet,
> Lie 'fore Bride and Bridegroom's feet,
>   Blessing their sense ;
> Not an angel of the air,
> Bird melodious or bird fair,
>   Is absent hence.
>
> The crow, the slanderous cuckoo, nor
> The boding raven, nor chough hoar,
>   Nor chatting pie,
> May on our bride-house perch or sing,
> Or with them any discord bring,
>   But from it fly.

Whether Beaumont withdrew entirely in 1611, or
lingered on until 1613, his influence seems to be very
slight in the second period of the collaborated plays.
Fletcher may have used hints supplied by his friend, but
in the main the plays of the last years of Beaumont's life
seem to be exclusively Fletcher's. In 1612 he probably
brought out *The Captain.* In 1613 *The Honest Man's*

Fortune and *The Nice Valour.* In 1614 *The Night-Walker, Wit without Money, The Woman's Prize,* and *The Faithful Friend.* In 1615 *The Chances.* In 1616 *Bonduca, Valentinian,* and *The Bloody Brother.* In 1617 *The Knight of Malta* and *The Queen of Corinth.* In 1618 *The Mad Lover, The Loyal Subject,* and *The Humourous Lieutenant.* Of these sixteen plays there is not one which can be said to be so important, either poetically or dramatically, as several of the preceding series, nor did Fletcher fail, at a subsequent time, to rise to greater heights. The decline is so abrupt at first as to mark almost beyond question the sudden weakness produced by the withdrawal of Beaumont; Fletcher learned gradually, but not without difficulty, to stand alone. Here are one or two good tragedies—*Bonduca, The Bloody Brother*—but not a single comedy, unless it be *The Chances,* which can be ranked among the best of Fletcher's. Aubrey's phrase, repeated from Earle, that Beaumont's "main business was to correct the over-flowings of Mr. Fletcher's wit," has often been quoted; but, in the presence of the phenomenon before us, it cannot be credited. Something very much more positive than a mere critical exercise of judgment was removed when Beaumont ceased to write, and the versification alone is enough to assure us of the abundance of his actual contributions. The prose-scenes in the plays of the earliest period were undoubtedly Beaumont's, and they testify to a vein of fancy very different from Fletcher's. It is noticeable, however, that this group of imperfect plays contains almost all Fletcher's most exquisite and imperishable songs.

In *Bonduca*, a romance of Roman Britain, Fletcher composed a tragedy which only just missed greatness, in the manner of Shakespeare. The patriot queen is well contrasted with the soldierly graces of Caratach. *The Bloody Brother* was greatly admired throughout the seventeenth century; Dryden described it as the only English tragedy " whose plot has that uniformity and unity of design in it which I have commended in the French," but to a modern taste it seems crude and harsh. *Valentinian*, another early favourite, told the story of Nero under the guise of new names and intrigues. This class of tragedies revealed the existence of masculine qualities of writing in Fletcher, and were composed with spirit and fervour. He was, however, to attain greater sureness of execution, and the plots of these melodramas display the results of haste and want of judgment. The individual speeches, and some scenes, possess great beauty; the general texture is improbable and disagreeable. The comedies of this group are marked by a sort of frenzied gaiety which is almost delirious, and which too frequently degenerates into horseplay. They seem all farce and whimsies, decked out, to be sure, in laces and ribands of very pretty poetry, but essentially volatile.

At the very moment when we become certain that the judgment of Beaumont was completely withdrawn from censuring the productions of his friend, we are aware that another talent is summoned to Fletcher's assistance. About 1619 Philip Massinger, an Oxford man of mature years, adopted the profession of dramatist, and began to work in conjunction with Fletcher. The circumstances of his life will be dealt with in a later chapter, when we come to treat his independent work. It is certain that at first he aimed at nothing more ambitious than the alteration and the completion of the plays of others. His collaboration seems not merely to have been welcome to Fletcher, but extremely stimulating, and for two years he and Massinger wrote with great assiduity a group of plays which appear in the so-called Beaumont-and-Fletcher collection. The main plays of this conjectural third group (1619-20) are *Sir John van Olden Barnaveldt*, *The Laws of Candy*, *The Custom of the Country*, *The Double Marriage*, *The Little French Lawyer*, *The False One*, *Women Pleased*, and *A Very Woman*. Of these there is little to be said for the five first, in which Fletcher strikes us as careless and Massinger still timid. The three last deserve separate attention.

In *The False One*, which deals with the familiar story of Antony and Cleopatra, the oratorical poetry of Fletcher rises to its sublimest altitude. The action of the piece is slow, and we are constantly tempted to regret Shakespeare's magnificent evolution. But of the grasp of character, the elevated conception of the principal figures, and the charm of broad and melodious poetry thrown like antique raiment about them, there can be no two opinions. *Women Pleased*, though the scene is laid in Florence, is a comedy of contemporary English life, full of agreeable humours. Bomby, the Puritan, who dances to "the pipe of persecution," and tries to stop the morris-dances, is a delightful creation, and is not too mechanically insisted on. The whole of the fourth act is very poetically conceived. *A Very*

Woman is now more commonly treated as mainly the work of Massinger.

According to Mr. Fleay's computation, the arrangement between Fletcher and Massinger was abruptly suspended from September, 1620, till March, 1622. If this be so, we may with a certain plausibility name a series of plays as having been written in those months by Fletcher unaided. These are *Monsieur Thomas, Thierry and Theodoret, The Island Princess, The Pilgrim*, and *The Wild Goose Chase.* It appears, at all events, that no hand but Fletcher's was at work on these five plays, and they are of so high an excellence as to make us regret that his haste or his idleness led him so often to lean upon others, instead of trusting to his own admirable resources. *Thierry and Theodoret* is commonly admitted to be the best of Fletcher's tragedies. The childless King of France, who is warned to slay the first woman whom he meets proceeding at sunrise from the temple of Diana, is confronted with the veiled figure of his own beloved wife, Ordella. This Lamb considered to be the finest scene in Fletcher, and Ordella his " most perfect idea of the female heroic character." *The Wild Goose Chase,* in like manner, is one of the brightest and most coherent of Fletcher's comedies, a play which it is impossible to read and not be in a good humour. The central incident of *Monsieur Thomas,* a middle-class Don Juan brought to summary justice, is too gross for modern readers; but the play is admirably worked out as a comical conception, and adorned with a bevy of pleasing and indignant girls.

The final group of the plays which are commonly bound

up together as the works of Beaumont and Fletcher is
the most difficult to arrange and appreciate. Massinger
may have returned to Fletcher in 1622, and may have
been concerned that year in *The Prophetess, The Sea
Voyage, The Spanish Curate,* and *The Beggar's Bush.*
Of these the last alone is important; it is a very odd
play, full of curious and fantastic stuff, and has had
warm admirers. Coleridge said of *The Beggar's Bush,*
"I could read it from morning to night; how sylvan and
sunshiny it is!" It is a Flemish comedy, in which the
ragged regiment are introduced using their cant phrases
and discovering their cozening tricks. In 1623 Fletcher
seems to have joined with some one who was not
Massinger, but whom it would be hazardous to name
with certainty, in writing *Wit at Several Weapons* and
The Maid of the Mill, the first an English, and the
second a Spanish comedy, trembling on the borderland
of farce.

At this point the career of Fletcher becomes in-
distinct to us, but it is very interesting to observe
that his genius seems to have deepened and brightened
to the last, for his very latest plays, probably produced
in 1624, are second to nothing of the same kind
written through the long course of his career. These
are the comedies of *A Wife for a Month,* and *Rule
a Wife and Have a Wife.* These are much less
farcical than the comic pieces which had preceded them,
and rest on a solid basis of invention. When the poet
composed *Rule a Wife and Have a Wife,* he must have
been worn with a career of persistent and laborious invention, yet nowhere in the mass of his voluminous

writings is the wit more fresh, the language more exquisite, elastic, and unexpected, or the evolution of character more delicate.

We may be permitted to hope that his anxieties were relaxed for some months before his death. But all we know is what Aubrey has retailed, that Fletcher died of the plague on the 19th of August, 1625, and that, "staying for a suit of clothes before he retired into the country, Death stopped his journey and laid him low." He was buried in the Church of St. Saviour's, Southwark, in a grave which was opened fourteen years later to receive Philip Massinger. The epitaph of Sir Aston Cockayne relates that—

> Plays they did write together, were great friends,
> And now one grave includes them in their ends ;
> Two whom on earth nothing could part, beneath
> Here in their fame they live, in spite of death.

Aubrey relates of Beaumont and Fletcher that " they lived together on the Bankside, not far from the playhouse, both bachelors, had the same clothes, cloak, etc., between them." Fuller tells a story of their joint composition, probably in some tavern, and the ejaculation, " I'll kill the king," being overheard and mistaken for high treason against James I.

The aims which actuated Beaumont and Fletcher were so lofty, and their actual performance so huge in extent, and uniformly ambitious in effort, that we are bound to judge them by no standard less exacting than the highest. Their resolute intention was to conquer a place in the very forefront of English literature, and for a time they seemed unquestionably to have succeeded in so doing. For a generation after the death of Fletcher, it might reasonably be mooted whether any British writer of poetry had excelled them. After the Restoration, although their popularity continued, their reputation with the critics began to decline, and no one will again name them with poets of the first class. They take, and will retain, an honourable position in the second rank, but in the first they can never again be placed. The conditions of their time seriously affected them. The highest point of poetic elevation had been reached, and the age, brilliant as it was, was one of decadence. It would have been possible to Beaumont and Fletcher— as still later on, when the incline was still more rapid, it yet was to Milton—to resist the elements of decay, to be pertinaciously distinguished, austere, and noble. But they had not enough strength of purpose for this; they gave way to the stream, and were carried down it, contenting themselves with flinging on it, from full hands, profuse showers of lyrical blossoms. They had to deal with a public which had cultivated a taste for the drama, and liked it coarse, bustling, and crude. They made it their business to please this public, not to teach or lead it, and the consequence was that they sacrificed to the whimsies of the pit all the proprieties, intellectual, moral, and theatrical.

It is a testimony to the talents of Beaumont and Fletcher that we do not compare them with any one but Shakespeare. Yet this is a test which they endure with difficulty. There are many scenes in which the superficial resemblance is so striking that we cannot hesitate to suppose that they were writing in conscious rivalry with their greatest contemporary. But it would be hard to point to a single instance in which he had not a complete advantage over them. They move too suddenly or too slowly, they are too fantastic for nature, or too flat for art, they are " making up," while he seems simply painting straight from the heart. It may perhaps be said, without injustice to Beaumont and Fletcher, that they differ from Shakespeare in this, that he is true throughout, and in relation to all the parts of the piece, while they are satisfied if they are true in isolated instances. Their single studies of a passion are often just and valuable in themselves, but they are almost always false to the combination in which the poets place them. What could be fairer or more genuine than the virtuous enthusiasm of Leucippus, what more unnatural and ridiculous in relation to the other personages which animate the tragedy of *Cupid's Revenge*?

The great twin-brethren of Jacobean poetry have many tricks which sink into conventions, and soon cease to please us. The incessant masquerade of girls as men, and boys as maidens, is one of them; we are fortunate when the girl disguised as a man (and, of course, acted, in those days, by a boy), does not assume a still further disguise as a woman. Beaumont and Fletcher's violent statement of moral problems which they have not the imagination nor the knowledge of the heart needful to unravel is a constant source of weakness; the looseness of their desultory plots, their hasty scheme in which, as Hazlitt has said, "everything seems in a state of fermentation and effervescence," their brazen recommendation of purely sensuous forces, their terrible facility and carelessness —all these are qualities which hold them back when they attempt the highest things, and it is sadly true that these eminent poets and all-accomplished playwrights have not left a single play which can be called first-rate.

If, however, Beaumont and Fletcher are severely judged at the strictest literary tribunal, they are none the less poets of an admirable excellence. Coleridge wished that they had written none but non-dramatic poetry, an expression, no doubt, of his sense of the beauty and propriety of their serious verse as compared with the meretricious rattle of what they designed to tickle the groundlings. It is not merely that their lyrics—their songs and masques and dirges—are so peculiarly exquisite, but that their soliloquies, for pure poetry, are unsurpassed in English dramatic literature. The poetry does not always seem in place, nor does it aid the evolution of the scenes, but in itself, in its relaxed and palpitating beauty, its sweetness of the hothouse, it is a delicious thing. The germs of the ruin of English prosody, of the degeneracy of English fancy, are in it, and they soon begin to fructify, but in the meantime the perfumed exotic is charming. Few dramatists can be quoted from with so much effect as Beaumont and Fletcher, or in that form are more enticing, or excite curiosity more acutely. The air they breathe is warm and musky, their star is " Venus, laughing with appeased desire," to young readers they appear divinely satisfying and romantically perfect. But deeper study does not further endear them, and the adult reader turns from them, with regret, to cultivate sterner and purer students of the heart. They are not quiet enough; we weary of their incessant "tibia orichalco vincta," and turn to simpler and serener masters. Yet even in their noisiness and their turbidity they were children of their age, and, when all is said, they were of the brood of the giants.

It may be convenient to deal at this point with a dramatist who was brought into intimate and constant relations with Beaumont and Fletcher, as an interpreter of their plays and as an occasional collaborator. Of Nathaniel Field we form a more definite notion than of any of the other minor playwrights of his time. We possess at Dulwich a striking portrait of him, and the incidents of his career are well defined. He was born in London in October, 1587, his father dying six months later. In 1597 the child was apprenticed to a stationer, being meanwhile educated at Merchant Taylors' School; but at twelve years of age we find that he was taken away to be an actor. In this capacity he came under the notice of Ben Jonson, who deigned to make the boy his scholar, and to read Horace and Martial with him. Field grew up with the instincts of a man of letters, and was proud of having acquired Latin. For the next ten years he played women's parts incessantly in the dramas of his great contemporaries, occasionally writing verses of his own. At length, in 1612, he published an independent play, *A Woman is a Weathercock*, which had probably been acted two years before. This must have been immediately followed by *Amends for Ladies*, which, however, was not published until 1618. Field wrote a third play, *The Fatal Dowry*, which Massinger completed and published in 1632.

Field was admitted to the Stationers' Company in
1611, and seems to have intended then to become a
publisher. He carried out this design some years later,
but remained upon the stage until about 1619. Chapman
was his poetic "father," and Field seems to have won
the affection of his associates. Of the close of his life
nothing is known except that he was buried on the 20th
of February, 1633. Field's two comedies are productions
of very considerable excellence, composed with solid art,
and combining some of the classic strength of Ben
Jonson with the sparkle and bustle of Fletcher. Field
is careful to preserve the unity of time. His *A Woman
is a Weathercock* is a satire on the volatility of the sex ;
in *Amends for Ladies*, as the title indicates, the author
shows how firm a woman can on occasion remain. The
second play, which is the better of the two, was enlivened by topical allusions to Moll Cutpurse, "the
Roaring Girl," who was doing penance at Paul's Cross
when the play was brought out. She was a favourite
character with the Jacobean dramatists. In *The Fatal
Dowry* Field attempted tragedy, and wrote the lugubrious
story of the unburied Charalois with dignity and pathos.

CHAPTER V.

IN this chapter we deal with certain poets, of very varied excellence, in whom the tradition of Elizabeth survived, although not in the Spenserian form. It may be convenient to begin with one who has been till lately almost unknown, but who, since 1889, and under the auspices of Mr. A. H. Bullen, has come to take his place at the forefront of the lyrical poets of the beginning of the seventeenth century. Of the exquisite genius of Thomas Campion there must in future be allowed no question. He was born about 1567, belonged in early youth to the society of Gray's Inn, practised as a physician, and ended as a professional musician. He published a volume of Latin epigrams in 1595. But it was not until 1601 that his first *Book of Airs* appeared, the forerunner of successive volumes of lyric verse set to music. He wrote a masque for Sir James Hay's wedding in 1607, and three more of these entertainments in 1613. Two *Books of Airs* appeared in 1610, and two more in 1612. It is from these publications, and from the song-books of his contemporaries, that Mr.

Bullen has collected the rich harvest of Campion's poetical works.

One of Campion's acute friends observed of his "happy lyrics" that they were "strained out of art by nature so with ease." These words very well express the adroit and graceful distinction which marks his verse. His taste was at once classical and romantic. So classical was it, that for a while he was beguiled away from rhyme altogether, and gave the sanction of his delicate accomplishment to those who, like the earlier Areopagites, desired to do away with the ornament of rhyme, and to write pure English sapphics and alcaics. Fortunately, this erroneous judgment did not prevail, and Campion returned to those numbers in which he had so eminent a skill.

His knowledge of music and the exigencies of the airs to which he wrote, gave great variety and yet precision to his stanzaic forms and his rhyme-arrangements. In certain respects, he reminds us of Fletcher at his best, and as Fletcher was the younger man, it is probable that he wrote some of his lyrics under Campion's influence. But no other writer of the time arrived at anything approaching to Campion's throbbing melody in such pieces as that beginning—

> Follow your saint, follow with accents sweet,
> Haste your sad notes, fall at her flying feet,

or his quaint, extravagant grace, as in—

> I care not for these ladies,
>   That must be wooed and prayed :
> Give me kind Amaryllis,
>   The wanton country maid.

> Nature art disdaineth,
>   Her beauty is her own ;
>   Her when we court and kiss,
>   She cries " Forsooth, let go ! "
>   But when we come where comfort is,
>   She never will say " No ! "

or his unexpected turns of metre, as in—

> All you that will hold watch with love,
>   The fairy queen Proserpina
> Will make you fairer than Dione's dove ;
>   Roses red, lilies white,
>   And the clear damask hue
> Shall on your cheeks alight ;
>   Love will adorn you.

The songs of Campion are commonly of an airy, amatory kind, plaintive, fanciful, and sensuous. But not infrequently he strikes another key, and comes closer to the impassioned sincerity of Donne. The following song, from the first *Book of Airs*, is of a very high quality—

> When thou must home to shades of underground,
>   And there arrived, a new admirèd guest,
> The beauteous spirits do engirt thee round,
>   White Iopë, blithe Helen, and the rest,
> To hear the stories of thy finished love,
> From that smooth tongue whose music hell can move ;
>
> Then wilt thou speak of banqueting delights,
>   Of masques and revels which sweet youth did make,
> Of tourneys and great challenges of knights,
>   And all those triumphs for thy beauty's sake ;
> When thou hast told these honours done to thee,
> Then tell, O tell, how thou didst murder me.

This may naturally be put by the side of "The Apparition" of Donne.

The four existing masques of Campion are skilful and gorgeous; they would be the best in English, if we could exclude the rich repertory of Ben Jonson. They give us an opportunity of judging that Campion would, had he chosen to do so, have excelled in the more elaborate kinds of poetry. His heroic verse, especially in the *Lords' Masque*, is full and stately, and deformed by none of those crabbed distortions of accentuation which many of his contemporaries affected. Campion's *Observations in the Art of English Poetry*, published in 1602, is a learned treatise on prosody, which has been unduly neglected. None of the experiments which it contains, however,—neither its "iambic dimetre," nor its "anacreontic licentiate—" are fit to compare with the author's more conventional rhymed verse. If an exception is to be found, it is perhaps in the following lyric, doubtless the most successful copy of unrhymed measure which that age produced—

> Rose-cheeked Laura, come ;
> Sing thou smoothly with thy beauty's
> Silent music, either other
> Sweetly gracing.
>
> Lovely forms do flow
> From concert divinely framèd ;
> Heav'n is music, and thy beauty's
> Birth is heavenly.
>
> These dull notes we sing,
> Discords need for helps to grace them,
> Only beauty purely loving,
> Knows no discord ;

But still moves delight,
Like clear springs renewed by flowing,
Ever perfect, ever in them-
    selves eternal.

Campion died early in 1620, and was buried in the
Church of St. Dunstan's in the West, in London.

If Campion has hitherto been neglected, the poet of
whom we have next to treat has enjoyed for two
hundred years past a popularity, or, at least, a nominal
prominence, which is somewhat in excess of his merits.
During the eighteenth century, at least, no non-dramatic
poet of our period was so much read or so often reprinted as Drayton. Joseph Hunter expressed no
opinion shocking to his generation when he claimed for
Drayton a place in the first class of English poets. His
ease, correctness, and lucidity were attractive to our
elder critics, and outweighed the lack of the more
exquisite qualities of style. If Drayton can no longer be
awarded such superlative honours as were formerly paid to
him, he is nevertheless a poet of considerable originality
and merit, whose greatest enemy has been his want of
measure. His works form far too huge a bulk, and
would be more gladly read if the imagination in them
were more concentrated and the style more concise.
Drayton attempted almost every variety of poetic art,
and his aim was possibly a little too encyclopædic for
his gifts.

It is impossible to yield to Drayton the position in
this volume which his pretensions demand, since a very
important portion of his work lies entirely outside our
scope. His career is divided into two distinct halves,

and the former of these, as purely Elizabethan, calls for
no detailed consideration here. Michael Drayton was
born near Atherstone, in Warwickshire, in 1563. He
came up to town while still a young man, and in the
last decade of Elizabeth produced divine poems, sonnets
in the fashion of the hour, pastorals, and, above all, certain
epical studies in historical poetry, which were akin in
nature to those produced during so long a period, and
in such diverse manners, by the versifiers of the *Mirror
for Magistrates.* He was forty years of age when
James I. came to the throne, and was already one of the
most prominent poets of the age.

Drayton's earliest act in the new reign was an unfortunate one. He hastened to be the first welcomer
in the field, and hurried out *A Gratulatory Poem to
King James.* His zeal, however, went beyond his
discretion; he was told that he should have waited
until the mourning for the queen was over, and the new
king refused to patronize him. Henceforth, a petulant
note is discernible in Drayton's writings, the note of dis-
appointment and disillusion. He was exceedingly active,
however, and brought out, in quick succession, fresh
and greatly revised editions of his old historical poems,
The Baron's Wars, and *England's Heroical Epistles.* A
new didactic and religious piece, *Moses in a Map of his
Miracles*, 1604, added little to his reputation; but the
Owl, of the same year, is a lengthy and important composition in the heroic couplet. The writer feigns, in
the mediæval manner, that he fell asleep under a tree
on a May morning, and heard all the birds talk-
ing in human speech. The opening of the poem is

of a Chaucerian prettiness. Among those birds who speak—

> The little Redbreast teacheth charity,

but the Linnet and the Titmouse presently twit the Owl on his silence, and the fiercer birds fall upon him with beak and claw. They would kill him, did not the Falcon protect him, and the Eagle come swooping down to see what is the matter. Then the Owl speaks. He has looked through the windows of the Eagle's court, and seen all the evil that is done there. At last the Eagle, having listened to the Owl's long satire, flies away, and the Owl is applauded and comforted. This curious satirical fable has passages of great merit; among them is this pathetic episode of the Crane :—

> Lo, in a valley peopled thick with trees,
> Where the soft day continual evening sees,
> Where, in the moist and melancholy shade,
> The grass grows rank, but yields a bitter blade,
> I found a poor Crane sitting all alone,
> That from his breast sent many a throbbing groan ;
> Grov'lling he lay, that sometime stood upright ;
> Maimed of his joints in many a doubtful fight ;
> His ashy coat that bore a gloss so fair,
> So often kiss'd of the enamour'd air,
> Worn all to rags, and fretted so with rust,
> That with his feet he trod it in the dust ;
> And wanting strength to bear him to the springs,
> The spiders wove their webs e'en in his wings.

Probably in 1606, Drayton issued one of the most charming of his books, *Poems Lyric and Pastoral,* consisting of odes, eclogues, and a curious romance called *The Man in the Moon.* The Odes doubtless belong to his youth ; they are particularly happy in their varied

versification, of which two brief specimens may suffice.
This stanza exemplifies the " Ode on the New Year "—

> Give her the Eoan brightness,
> Wing'd with that subtle lightness,
>   That doth transpierce the air ;
> The roses of the morning,
> The rising heaven adorning,
>   To mesh with flames of hair.

and this the " Ode to his Valentine "—

> Muse, bid the morn awake,
>   Sad winter now declines,
> Each bird doth choose a make,
>   This day's Saint Valentine's.
> For that good bishop's sake,
>   Get up and let us see,
>   What beauty it shall be,
> That fortune us assigns.

These are fresh and lively, without any strong grip
on thought. By far the best of the odes, however, is
the noble *Battle of Agincourt,* which is Drayton's greatest
claim to the recognition of posterity, and the most
spirited of all his lyrics.

In a bold preface to his " Eclogues," Drayton promises
something new ; but these pastorals are not to be distinguished from Elizabethan work of the same kind, except
by the fine lyrics which are introduced in the course of
them. Of these the best is the very remarkable birthday
ode to Beta in the third eclogue—

> Stay, Thames, to hear my song, thou great and famous flood,
> Beta alone the phœnix is of all thy watery brood,
>   The queen of virgins only she,
>   The king of floods allotting thee

Of all the rest, be joyful thou to see this happy day,
Thy Beta now alone shall be the subject of thy lay.

With dainty and delightsome strains of dapper virelays,
Come, lovely shepherds, sit by me, to tell our Beta's praise;
    And let us sing so high a verse
    Her sovereign virtues to rehearse,
That little birds shall silent sit to hear us shepherds sing,
Whilst rivers backwards bend their course, and flow up to their spring.

Range all thy swans, fair Thames, together on a rank,
And place them each in their degree upon thy winding bank,
    And let them set together all,
    Time keeping with the waters' fall,
And crave the tuneful nightingale to help them with her lay,
The ouzel and the throstle-cock, chief music of our May.

   *   *   *   *   *

Sound loud your trumpets then from London's loftiest towers
To beat the stormy tempests back, and calm the raging showers,
    Set the cornet with the flute,
    The orpharion to the lute,
Tuning the tabor and the pipe to the sweet violins,
And mock the thunder in the air with our loud clarions.

For the rest, these pieces present a vague but pretty impression of nymphs singing and dancing in the flowery meadows around a middle-aged swain who deplores to them his want of material success and courtly recognition.

Passing, for the moment, the *Poly-Olbion*, we come in 1627 to a miscellaneous volume, consisting of seven independent poetical works not before given to the public. Of these two, *The Battle of Agincourt* (not to be confounded with the ode) and *The Miseries of Queen Margaret*, are fragments of that epic in *ottava rima* which Drayton was always projecting and never completed. *Nimphidia, or the Court of Fairy*, is a fantastic little romance, perhaps closer to being a masterpiece than any other which Drayton composed, dealing with the loves of Pigwiggin and Queen Mab in a style of the most airy fancy. *The Moon-Calf* is as clumsy as its predecessor is elegant and exquisite ; this is a kind of coarse satirical fable in the heroic couplet. *The Quest of Cinthia* is a long ballad, so smooth, and it must be confessed, so conventional, that it might almost have been written a century and a half later. *The Shepherd's Sirena* is a lyric pastoral of much lightness and charm, and the volume closes with some *Elegies* of various merit.

At least as early as 1598, as we learn from Francis Meres, Drayton had designed a heroic and patriotic poem of great extent. It was to celebrate the kingdom of Great Britain with the exactitude of Camden, but with the addition of every species of imaginative ornament. At length, in 1613, a folio appeared, entitled *Poly-Olbion*, "a chorographical description of tracts, rivers, mountains, forests, and other parts of this renowned isle." This original instalment contained eighteen "Songs" or cantos, and was enriched by copious notes from the pen of John Selden, and a map to each "song." *Poly-Olbion* was reissued in 1622, with twelve new cantos, but Selden contributed no more notes.

As the poet says, the composition of *Poly-Olbion* was "a Herculean toil," and it was one which scarcely rewarded the author. He had a great difficulty in finding a publisher for the complete work, and he told the sympathetic Drummond—"my dear sweet Drummond"—that the booksellers were "a company of base knaves."

The work is written in a couplet of twelve-syllable iambic lines, in imitation of the French Alexandrine, but with an unfailing cœsura after the third foot, which becomes very tiresome to the ear.

As an example of the method of the poem, may be selected the passage in which Drayton describes the habits of the aboriginal beaver of South Wales—

> More famous long agone than for the salmons' leap,
> For beavers Tivy was, in her strong banks that bred,
> Which else no other brook in Britain nourishèd ;
> Where Nature, in the shape of this now-perish'd beast,
> His property did seem to have wondrously expressed ;
> Being bodied like a boat, with such a mighty tail
> As serv'd him for a bridge, a helm, or for a sail,
> When kind did him command the architect to play,
> That his strong castle built of branchèd twigs and clay ;
> Which, set upon the deep, but yet not fixèd there,
> He easily could remove as it he pleas'd to steer
> To this side or to that ; the workmanship so rare,
> His stuff wherewith to build, first being to prepare,
> A foraging he goes, to groves or bushes nigh,
> And with his teeth cuts down his timber; which laid by,
> He turns him on his back,—his belly laid abroad,—
> When with what he hath got, the others do him load,
> Till lastly, by the weight, his burden he hath found ;
> Then with his mighty tail his carriage having bound
> As carters do with ropes, in his sharp teeth he gript
> Some stronger stick, from which the lesser branches stript,
> He takes it in the midst ; at both the ends, the rest
> Hard holding with their fangs, unto the labour prest,
> Going backward, tow'rds their home their laded carriage led,
> From whom those first here born were taught the useful sled.

At the same time, it must be confessed that the entire originality of the poem, its sustained vivacity, variety and accuracy, and its unlikeness to any other work of the age, give an indubitable interest to *Poly-Olbion*, which will always be referred to with pleasure, though seldom followed from " the utmost end of Cornwall's furrowing beak," to the fall of Esk and Eden into the Western Sands.

The confidence of Drayton in his own divine mission is sublime and pathetic. However unlucky he may be, he invariably takes the attitude of a poet of unquestioned eminence. In his *Man in the Moon*, the shepherds give Rowland (Drayton's accepted pseudonym) the office of their spokesman, because he was—

> By general voice, in times that then was grown,
> So excellent, that scarce there had been known,
> Him that excell'd in piping or in song.

His popularity might account for, yet scarcely excuse this attitude; but, in spite of this egotism, Drayton is a writer who commands our respect. He is manly and direct, and his virile style has the charm of what is well-performed in an easy and straightforward manner. He had studied the earlier poets to good effect. His critical knowledge of literature was considerable, and his acquaintance with natural objects exceptionally wide. His vocabulary is rich and uncommon; he has a pleasing preference for technical and rustic words. His variety, his ambition, his excellent versification claim our respect and admiration; but Drayton's weak point is that he fails to interest his reader. All is good, but little is superlatively entertaining. His most perfect poem was introduced by him, without any special attention being drawn to it, in what is supposed to be

the sixth edition of his *Poems*, the folio of 1619.   It is
the following touching and passionate sonnet :—

> Since there's no help, come let us kiss and part, —
> Nay, I have done, you get no more of me ;
> And I am glad, yea glad with all my heart,
> That thus so cleanly I myself can free.
>
> Shake hands for ever, cancel all our vows,
> And when we meet at any time again,
> Be it not seen in either of our brows,
> That we one jot of former love retain.
>
> Now at the last gasp of love's latest breath,
> When, his pulse failing, passion speechless lies,
> When, faith is kneeling by his bed of death,
> And innocence is closing up his eyes,—
>
> —Now if thou wouldst, when all have given him over,
> From death to life thou mightst him yet recover !

Drayton continued to write and to publish verses after
the death of James I., and did not until the 23rd of
December, 1631, as his monument in Poet's Corner has
it, "exchange his laurel for a crown of glory."   Ben
Jonson, who had not appreciated Drayton in his lifetime,
is said to have composed the epitaph graven in letters of
gold beneath his bust in Westminster Abbey.

Poetry had greatly declined in Scotland when James
VI. became James I. of England.   The monarch himself, although in his own esteem more than a prentice
in the divine art, abandoned the practice of poetry on
coming south.   There remained, among his northern
subjects, but one poet of really commanding excellence,
William Drummond of Hawthornden, a youth at that
time still unknown to fame.   Drummond belonged to

the class of artistic or cultivated poets, to that which is made by literature rather than born of spontaneous creation. In the earliest of his sonnets, Drummond admits as much :—" I first began to read, then loved to write." But among poets of this studious and literary kind, he ranks very high indeed. He possesses style, distinction, a practised and regulated skill, in a degree denied to many of his more spontaneously gifted fellows. It would be a grave error, in any estimate of Jacobean poetry, to underrate this admirable poetic artist.

William Drummond was born of ancient Scottish lineage on the 13th of December, 1585. Upon his taking his degree in Edinburgh in 1605, he was sent to the Continent, and after a twelvemonth spent in learning law at Bourges, he seems to have resided three years in Paris. This residence has left its imprint on his writings. In Paris, at that time, Ronsard, who had died the year Drummond was born, was still regarded as an almost unquestioned master ; Pontus de Tyard, last survivor of the Pléiade, was only just dead. It is strange if the young Scotchman did not meet with the vigorous Agrippa d'Aubigné, a Protestant and Ronsardist like himself, for Drummond fell immediately into the manner of the Pléiade. No one in English, except the feebler Barnaby Barnes, was so Gallic as Drummond, whose best pieces might have been translated into French of the beginning of the seventeenth century without raising any suspicion of a foreign influence.

In 1609 the young man returned to Edinburgh, and in 1610 withdrew to his romantic and now classic estate of Hawthornden. In 1613 the death of Prince Henry drew from him an elegy, his earliest published work, the *Tears on the Death of Moeliades*, an artificial and extremely Ronsardist poem in couplets of considerable mellifluousness, closing thus—

> For ever rest ! Thy praise fame may enroll
> In golden annals, whilst about the pole
> The slow Boötes turns, or sun doth rise,
> With scarlet scarf to cheer the mourning skies ;
> The virgins to thy tomb may garlands bear
> Of flowers, and on each flower let fall a tear.
> Moeliades sweet courtly nymphs deplore,
> From Thule to Hydaspes' pearly shore.

Three years later Drummond issued a slender volume of *Poems*, consisting of sonnets, odes, sextains, and madrigals. His notion of the madrigal was a small irregular lyric, opening with a six-syllable iambic line. This is a characteristic specimen—

> This life, which seems so fair,
> Is like a bubble blown up in the air
> By sporting children's breath,
> Who chase it everywhere,
> And strive who can most motion it bequeath ;
> And though it sometime seem of its own might,
> Like to an eye of gold, to be fix'd there,
> And firm to hover in that empty height,
> That only is because it is so light.
> But in that pomp it doth not long appear ;
> For even when most admir'd, it, in a thought,
> As swell'd from nothing, doth dissolve in naught.

His sonnets, a form in which he is peculiarly successful, approach more nearly to perfection of rhyme-structure than any of those of his contemporaries, except perhaps Donne's; but he is rarely able to resist the tempting

error of the final couplet.   One or two long and glowing
odes of great merit he styles " songs."   This first collection of his poems contains many lyrics that are admirable, and few that are without dignity and skill.   He
uses flowers and pure colours like a Tuscan painter, and
strikes us as most fantastic when he essays to write in
dispraise of beauty, since no poet of his time is so
resolute a worshipper of physical loveliness as he is.   In
Drummond's voluptuous and gorgeous verse there is no
trace of the Elizabethan *naïveté* or dramatic passion.
It is the deliberate poetry of an accomplished scholar-
artist.

As he grew older, Drummond became pious, but without
changing his style.   His *Flowers of Sion* of 1623 are
gnomic or moral, and not by any means exclusively
religious.   The famous sonnet to the Nightingale forms
a part of this volume :—

> Sweet bird, that sing'st away the early hours,
>   Of winter's past or coming void of care,
>   Well pleasèd with delights which present are,
> Fair seasons, budding sprays, sweet-smelling flowers ;
> To rocks, to springs, to rills, from leafy bowers
>   Thou thy Creator's goodness doth declare,
>   And what dear gifts on thee he did not spare,
> A stain to human sense in sin that lowers.
> What soul can be so sick which by thy songs,
>   Attir'd in sweetness, sweetly is not driven
> Quite to forget earth's turmoils, spites and wrongs,
>   And lift a reverend eye and thought to heaven?
> Sweet artless songster, thou my mind dost raise
> To airs of spheres, yes, and to angels' lays.

What are most remarkable, from the point of view
of style, among these divine poems, are certain can-

zonets in which there is found such a sensuous ardour
and fiery perfume as were not to be met with again
in English religious verse until the days of Crashaw.
In "A Hymn to the Passion" we have one of the earliest,
if not the very earliest, lengthy exercise in *terza rima* in
our language, a *tour de force* carried out with surprising
ease. More spirited is the ode on the "Resurrection,"
and it might be difficult to overpraise, in its own elaborate
and glittering manner, the ode called "An Hymn of the
Ascension." It opens thus—

> Bright portals of the sky,
>   Emboss'd with sparkling stars,
>   Doors of eternity,
>   With diamantine bars,
>   Your arras rich uphold,
>   Loose all your bolts and springs,
>   Ope wide your leaves of gold,
>   That in your roofs may come the King of kings !
>
> Scarf'd in a rosy cloud,
>   He doth ascend the air ;
>   Straight doth the moon him shroud
>   With her resplendent hair ;
>   The next encrystall'd light
>   Submits to him its beams,
>   And he doth trace the height
>   Of that fair lamp whence flame of beauty streams.
>
> He towers those golden bounds
>   He did to sun bequeath ;
>   The higher wandering rounds
>   Are found his feet beneath ;
>   The Milky Way comes near,
>   Heaven's axle seems to bend
>   Above each turning sphere
>   That, rob'd in glory, heaven's King may ascend.

What Drummond says is never so important as the way in which he says it, and it would be as absurd to look for any spiritual fervour or record of deep experience in these *Flowers of Sion* as it would be to suppose them in any way disingenuous. The spangled style was the cassock which best suited the sincere but sensuous piety of this poetical preacher. To the *Flowers of Sion* was appended *The Cypress Grove*, a prose treatise to edification, containing some few sonnets, not the author's best.

In 1619 Ben Jonson came up to Hawthornden, and talked about his contemporaries. Of these conversations Drummond has preserved an invaluable report, bearing the fullest impress of veracity. The Scotch poet continued to write after the death of James I., and survived until 1649.

Of other Northern writers, Sir William Alexander, Earl of Stirling, will be treated in another place. Alexander Craig, of Rose-Craig (1567 ?–1627), was a sonneteer who possessed some measure of pedantic skill. His friend, Sir Robert Aytoun (1570–1638), was, like himself, a student of St. Leonard's College in St. Andrews. Aytoun long preserved a considerable reputation for the grace and delicacy of his verse; but, unhappily, a doubt hangs over his most admired compositions, and it is not certain that we possess, as his, the verses which Dryden pronounced "some of the best of that age." Robert Ker, Earl of Ancrum (1578–1654), was a sonneteer; and, finally, the Scotch include among their poets Alexander Garden (1587 ?–1645), who wrote *A Theatre of Scottish Worthies*, and other respectable volumes.

An English poet to whose merit justice has scarcely been done is Sir John Beaumont, the brother of Francis, the dramatist. He was writing verses during the whole of James I.'s reign, but he did not publish them, and some of his most important work has perished. He was born, the second son of Sir Thomas Beaumont, of Grace-dieu, in 1583, and was educated at Oxford. In the last year of Elizabeth an anonymous poem was printed in London, entitled *The Metamorphosis of Tobacco;* this is attributed to Sir John, and bears all the impress of his rather peculiar versification. He was made a baronet in 1626, and, dying in April, 1627, was buried in West-minster Abbey. His son, Sir John, a noted athlete, afterwards killed at the siege of Gloucester—himself an accomplished versifier—edited his father's posthumous works in 1629, as *Bosworth Field: with a Taste of the Variety of other Poems;* but Sir John Beaumont's pre-sumed masterpiece, his long religious poem of *The Crown of Thorns*, has disappeared, and may be regarded as a serious loss, for it was much admired by his con-temporaries.

The versification of Beaumont is remarkably polished. No one, indeed, was in 1602 writing the heroic couplet so "correctly" as the author of *The Metamorphosis*. This mock-heroic piece, which has been underestimated, is full of most charming fancies, and promises more than Sir John Beaumont ever quite carried out. *Bosworth Field* is a carefully, and again a very smoothly, written historical poem, but a little arid and cold, the theme being one beyond the author's powers, which tended to lose themselves in the desultory and the unessential.

This is a pathetic example of *Bosworth Field*—

> If, in the midst of such a bloody fight,
> The name of friendship be not thought too light,
> Recount, my Muse, how Byron's faithful love
> To dying Clifton did itself approve :
> For Clifton, fighting bravely in the troop,
> Receives a wound, and now begins to droop ;
> Which Byron seeing,—though in arms his foe,
> In heart his friend, and hoping that the blow
> Had not been mortal—guards him with his shield
> From second hurts, and cries, "Dear Clifton, yield !
> Thou hither cam'st, led by sinister fate,
> Against my first advice, yet now, though late,
> Take this my counsel !" Clifton thus replied :—
> "It is too late, for I must now provide
> To seek another life ; live thou, sweet friend !"

Beaumont's sacred and his courtly poems are lucid and graceful, without much force, the neatness of the tripping couplets being more remarkable than the freshness of the imagery.

The death of his son Gervase wrung from Sir John Beaumont this touching elegy—

> Can I, who have for others oft compiled
> The songs of death, forget my sweetest child,
> Which like a flower crushed, with a blast is dead,
> And ere full time hangs down his smiling head,
> Expecting with dear hope to live anew,
> Among the angels, fed with heavenly dew?
> We have this sign of joy, that, many days,
> While on the earth his struggling spirit stays,
> The name of Jesus in his mouth contains
> His only food, his sleep, his ease from pains.
> O may that sound be rooted in my mind,
> Of which in him such strong effect I find.
> Dear Lord, receive my son, whose winning love
> To me was like a friendship, far above

> The course of nature, or his tender age,—
> Whose looks could all my bitter grief assuage ;
> Let his pure soul ordain'd seven years to be
> In that frail body, which was part of me,
> Remain my pledge in heaven, as sent to show
> How to this port at every step I go.

So far as we can judge, he was curiously devoid of the lyrical tendency, and wrote little which was not in the couplet which he manipulated so cleverly.

Richard Brathwait was born, as it is believed, near Kendal, in 1588. He died at Catterick on May 4, 1673, being therefore in existence from the prime of Spenser's life until after the birth of Addison. He became a commoner of Oriel College, Oxford, in 1604, and, if we may believe his own words, about that time began the work that he was all his life polishing up, the *Barnabae Itinerarium*. Removing afterwards to Cam·bridge, he became a pupil of Lancelot Andrews, but distinguished himself more as an inveterate lover of dissolute company than as a student or a thinker. He married in 1617, became the captain of a foot-company of trained-bands, deputy-lieutenant of the county of Westmoreland, and a justice of the peace. The only other noticeable fact of his life was that he became the father of the gallant and unfortunate Sir Strafford Brathwait, who died fighting the Algerines. His works range from *The Golden Fleece*, published in 1611, to a sort of commentary on Chaucer, which appeared in 1665, and thus his literary life embraced more than half a century. His serious poems, elegies, odes, madrigals, and the like, are unredeemed dulness, the very flattest ditch-water imitations of such rare poets as Breton and Daniel ; but he had a genuine vein of boisterous humour, and this gives some doubtful value to a few vivacious pieces.

The *Barnabae Itinerarium*, however, is worthy of rather more definite praise than this, if only on the score of its novelty and oddity. It was printed in Latin and English, in a six-line rhymed stanza, the Latin on one side, the English on the other. As a feat of versification, the English version is distinctly remarkable, being written throughout in double rhymes. The meaning is usually more obvious and expressed more naturally in the Latin, and one may therefore surmise that this is the original text. The poem is divided into four books, each describing a distinct journey, and each probably composed at a different part of the author's life. All are ribald, but the first and most juvenile is peculiarly profligate and reckless. Inasmuch as we may take the recital as being autobiographical, it gives us the undisguised portrait of the poet as a drunken young ruffian. Praise of liquor is the great inspiring theme, and he worships Bacchus with the fervour of a devotee. " Jamais homme noble ne hayst le bon vin: c'est ung apophthegme monachal," says somebody in *Gargantua*, and Brathwait might have taken this axiom as his text.

> This way, that way, each way shrunk I,
> Little eat I, deeply drunk I,

he says, and his *Itinerary* is distinctly unedifying. Unamusing it is not. On the threshold we meet with a famous morsel of burlesque—

> In my progress travelling northward,
> Taking my farewell o' the southward,

> To Banbury came I, O profane one,
> Where I saw a Puritane one
> Hanging of his cat on Monday,
> For killing of a mouse on Sunday.

At Nottingham he finds highway riders still imitating the great deeds of Robin Hood and Little John; at Wakefield he is disappointed not to meet with the veritable Pinner, George-a-Green—

> Veni Wakefeeld peramoenum,
> Ubi quaerens Georgium Grenum,
> Non inveni.

At Ingleton, some women threw half a brick at him, in quite the modern manner. At Hodsdon he is prevailed on to play cards with some coney-catchers, who fleece him of everything; he has them up before a justice, but he is only jeered at for his pains. At Wansforth Briggs he has an odd adventure, which he thus recounts in his terse fashion—

> On a haycock sleeping soundly,
> Th' river rose and took me roundly
> Down the current; people cried;
> Sleeping, down the stream I hièd;
> "Where away," quoth they, "from Greenland?"
> "No! from Wansforth Briggs in England!"

His constant complaints of the accommodation he meets with are pathetic—

> Inns are nasty, dusty, fusty,
> Both with smoke and rubbish musty.

These quotations do not give an unfair idea of the best humour of a poem that never drags or becomes dull, but which is generally indecorous and always doggerel. It scarcely belongs to literature at all, but it deserves a place in every library that admits what is dedicated to whimsical humours.

Scarcely more poetical and not so amusing were the voluminous tractates of John Davies (1565—1618?), the writing-master of Hereford. Mr. Saintsbury has generously discovered in him " a certain salt of wit which puts him above the mere pamphleteers." But it requires a very strenuous effort to find savour in Davies, who is not to be confounded with the admirable Elizabethan poet of the *Nosce Teipsum*. He began with a philosophical *Mirum in Modum* in 1602, and closed his series of fifteen or sixteen publications with a *Wit's Bedlam* in 1617. Davies of Hereford deserves recognition of the same sort as may be awarded to Samuel Rowlands, whom in some respects he followed, if he did not imitate. His works are mines for the literary antiquarian, but defy the mere poetical reader.

The early metrical romances of Shakespeare found a not unskilful imitator in the actor William Barkstead, who published a *Mirrha* in 1607 and a *Hiren* in 1611. An anonymous writer selected the first of these themes for a poem called *The Scourge of Venus*, 1613, so closely similar in style to Barkstead's acknowledged work that it is a temptation, in spite of the repetition of subject, to suppose the writers identical. Barkstead's tribute to his great predecessor may be given as an example of his manner; *Mirrha* closes thus—

> But stay, my Muse, in thine own confines keep,
>   And make not war with so dear-loved a neighbour ;
> But, having sung thy day-song, rest and sleep,
>   Preserve thy small fame and his greater favour ;

His song was worthy merit ; Shakespeare, he
Sung the fair blossom, thou the withered tree ;
Laurel is due to him, his art and wit
Hath purchased it ; cypress thy brow will fit.

Barkstead, whose name is traditionally connected with
those of Peele and Marston, may have helped those
playwrights in their dramatic work.   He was not without
a reflection of the Elizabethan glow and voluptuousness
of style.

Certain still lesser figures may be rapidly marshalled
at the close of this chapter.   The actor and pamphleteer,
Robert Arnim, published in 1609 a lively doggerel poem,
called *The Italian Tailor and his Boy.*   Peter Woodhouse, of whom nothing is recorded, produced a strange
moral fable, or disguised satire, *The Elephant and the
Flea,* 1605.   Richard Niccols, born in 1584, was known
not merely as the final editor of *The Mirror for Magistrates* in 1610, to which edition he contributed " The
Fall of Princes," and " A Winter Night's Vision "—but
as the author of eight or nine independent volumes of
smooth and fluent verse, always readable enough, though
tame and uninspired.   Niccols' best work is his journal-
istic poem, called *Sir Thomas Overbury's Vision,* 1616,
a sort of rhymed "special edition" to be distributed
under the scaffold of the murderers.   Richard Middleton,
of York, published *Epigrams* in 1608, and Henry Parrot
several volumes of short satirical pieces, from *The
Mouse-Trap* of 1606 to *VIII. Cures for the Itch* in
1626.   Thomas Freeman, an Oxford graduate, came to
London, as Wood says, "to set up for a poet," and
published in 1614 *Rub and a Great Cast,* a volume of

epigrams, among which are some on Shakespeare and other leading poets of the age. Sir William Leighton, an unlucky knight who died in want, and perhaps in prison, about 1614, was both a versifier and a musician. So was John Daniel, the brother of the poet-laureate, who published *Songs for the Lute, Viol, and Voice,* in 1606.

This is one of Daniel's madrigals—

> Thou pretty bird, how do I see
> Thy silly state and mine agree !
> For thou a prisoner art ;
> So is my heart.
> Thou sing'st to her, and so do I address
> My music to her ear that's merciless ;
> But herein doth the difference lie,—
> That thou art grac'd, so am not I ;
> Thou singing liv'st, and I must singing die.

If it could be proved that Robert Jones was himself the author of the exquisite madrigals and seed-pearl of song which are found scattered through his numerous publications for the lute and the bass-viol, he would claim a place among the lyrical poets of the age only just below that assigned to Campion.

This is from Jones' *The Muses' Garden of Delights,* 1610—

> The sea hath many thousand sands,
>   The sun hath motes as many ;
> The sky is full of stars, and love
>   As full of woes as any ;
> Believe me, that do know the elf,
> And make no trial by thyself.

It is in truth a pretty toy
        For babes to play withal ;
But O the honies of our youth
        Are oft our age's gall !
Self-proof in time will make thee know
He was a prophet told thee so.

A prophet that, Cassandra-like,
        Tells truth without belief ;
For headstrong Youth will run his race,
        Although his goal be brief ;
Love's martyr, when his heart is fast,
Proves Care's confessor at the last.

The social prominence and mysterious murder of <u>Sir</u>
Thomas Overbury gave an exaggerated interest to his
brief posthumous exercise in verse, *A Wife*, 1614, and
to his version of Ovid's *Remedy of Love*, 1620. Overbury, who was an agreeable prose essayist, was born at
Compton Scorfen in 1581, and was poisoned with blue
vitriol at the instance of the infamous Countess of
Somerset in September, 1613. His poem, with the essays
attached to it, went through some twenty editions. One
stanza may be quoted here, as an example of its
manner—

Books are a part of man's prerogative,
        In formal ink they thoughts and voices hold,
That we to them our solitude may give,
        And make time-present travel that of old ;
Our life Fame pierceth longer at the end,
And books it further backward do extend.

CHAPTER VI.

HEYWOOD—MIDDLETON—ROWLEY.

THERE is no greater inconvenience for a writer of second-rate talent than to come before the public in the midst of a short and brilliant epoch, and to wear out the evening of his days when all his greatest contemporaries are gone. His colleagues surpass him when he is young, his juniors easily outstrip the labours of his middle-age, and he finds himself at last stranded on an unfriendly generation that has forgotten his first works and despises his last as effete. Something of this sad fatality seems to have attended the life of Heywood; he was elbowed by Shakespeare and Jonson at the outset of his career, and without having succeeded in fully arresting the attention of any one of the swiftly passing generations that he found place in, he died when Milton and Marvell were introducing a system of poetry in which he, and such as he, found no place whatever. He passed away unnoticed; no contemporary devoted a printed line to the death of a dramatist who remained completely unknown till Charles Lamb breathed fresh life into the Elizabethan valley of dry bones.

Since his resuscitation he has suffered from a fresh injustice, the cause of which it is not easy to discover. Those who have complained of his flatness, rudeness, want of poetic art, have themselves increased these qualities in tacitly considering him as one of the latest of the great dramatic group. He is usually placed in chronological arrangement after Massinger, after Ford, with only Shirley and Jasper Mayne behind him. It is true that he lived till all but these were gone, but not on that account ought he to be considered as one of the latest of the group. The proper position of Heywood is in the centre, at the climax of the drama. That miraculous decade (1590–1600) in which the green undergrowth of English literature, as if in a single tropical night, burst into wave after wave of sudden blossom, produced so much and developed so rapidly that the closest study is needed to detect the stages of poetic progress.

Heywood began to write for the stage about 1594, and took his place at once in distinct defiance to the school of Marlowe, seeing sooner than Shakespeare did, because dowered with an imagination infinitely less fervid, the dangers of that melodramatic style that fascinated to the last the more poetic members of the cycle. To the romanticism of Beaumont and Fletcher, men of a slightly later date than his, he did not become attracted until long afterwards, and with the tragic poets he never held any communion whatever. He remained to the last simple, old-fashioned and unsophisticated, and tried to palm off dramas full of the pre-Shakespearian *naïveté* and directness upon audiences accustomed to the morbid subtleties of Ford. At last, one knows not when, but probably not before 1650, this brave and contented spirit passed silently away.

Thomas Heywood, gentleman, was born in all probability about 1570, in Lincolnshire. He went to Cambridge and became fellow of Peterhouse ; while at the University he saw "tragedies, comedies, histories, pastorals, and shows publicly acted." About the year 1594 he was an actor in the Lord Admiral's Company ; and his connection with the stage lasted until about 1635. According to his own famous phrase, so often reprinted from *The English Traveller*, in 1633 the plays were in number "two hundred and twenty, in which I have had either an entire hand, or at least a main finger." It is exceedingly difficult to know in what "a main finger" consists. If it merely means that Heywood was in the habit of putting gag into all the plays in which he acted, the explanation is easy, but this is hardly possible. There still exist about forty dramatic pieces with which Heywood is identified. Some of his earliest works seem to have been dramas of considerable size dealing with the myths of classical antiquity, and these are so totally unlike Heywood's subsequent plays that it is difficult to realize their identity of authorship. Their value, however, as works of poetic art, is about the same. They are somewhat tamely and evenly unimaginative, reaching their highest elevation in crises of a certain picturesqueness. These, however, and the miscellaneous and doubtful plays which follow them, belong to the reign of Elizabeth.

Under James I., Heywood produced, about 1603, his famous domestic tragedy, *A Woman Killed with Kindness.*

Probably to the same period may be assigned *The
Rape of Lucrece*. The tragi-comedy of *Fortune by
Land and Sea*, in which Rowley had a hand, although
not published until 1655, belongs to this earlier period.
It is supposed that Heywood wrote about six plays
a year, and it is exceedingly hazardous even to con-
jecture the succession of those which have survived.
The Fair Maid of the West, The English Traveller,
and *Love's Mistress* are probably among the very latest.
When we have mentioned *The Royal King and the
Loyal Subject, The Lancashire Witches*, and *A Challenge
for Beauty*, we have named all the important plays of
Heywood which can possibly be considered Jacobean.

The remarks of Charles Lamb on Heywood are well
known. "Heywood," says Elia, "is a sort of prose
Shakespeare. His scenes are to the full as natural and
affecting. But we miss *the Poet*, that which in Shakespeare always appears out and above the surface of *the
nature*." Given thus in its amplification, the criticism,
if still a little too enthusiastic, is sound and intelligible.
But to speak casually of Heywood as a "prose Shakespeare" is to offer a stumbling-block to the feet of
inexperienced readers. It needs the imagination of a
Lamb to divine the one aspect in which it is possible
to read Shakespeare into Heywood. He is curiously
lacking in that distinction of temper which was so
frequent in his age. In studying most of the great men
of that time, we are forced in some measure to lift
ourselves into their altitudes in order to enjoy their
qualities. The humours of Ben Jonson, the funereal
silences of Webster, the frenzies of Middleton, the

romantic intoxication of Fletcher—these are conditions of the imagination with which our modern life is little in sympathy, and to throw ourselves cordially into them we must resolutely forget the habits of thought which chequer our modern daily life. It is not so with what is most characteristic in Heywood. No effort is needed to make the spirit in sympathy with him. This mild and genial nature knew nothing of the subtle mysteries of human experience, and satisfied himself with presenting before us such simple and realistic pictures as shall move us to quiet laughter and passing tears. As a history of domestic sorrow, nobly borne by the wronged, and bitterly atoned by the wrong-doer, without heroic circumstances and without high-flown phrases, *A Woman Killed with Kindness* remains unexcelled, perhaps unequalled, in our poetical literature. It is the most highly finished of the dramas of Heywood, and the only one which has been put on the stage within recent times. It was first published in 1607.

When Heywood came to write *The English Traveller* he was more under the influence of Ben Jonson than of Shakespeare. His language has here lost its simple and straightforward character; it is full of quips and catches, and the dialogue is studded with conceited oaths. The plot of this play is founded on that of the *Mostellaria* of Plautus, and the really affecting scenes of it deal with the unselfish love of an old gentleman, recently wedded to a young wife, for one of the fine young men that become so familiar to readers of Heywood. He trusts the youth with his house, wealth, and wife, secure in his known honour; but sorrow is brought on all the characters by

the heartless intrigues of a friend whom the young man
introduces into his old host's house. This play is full of
clever and picturesque passages, and there is in particular
one describing a riotous party of drinking men, which is
perhaps the most spirited page of Heywood's writing. The
Shakespearian qualities of sweetness and gentleness which
Charles Lamb has claimed for this author are pleasantly
exemplified in *The Challenge for Beauty*, a Spanish story
of the love of Petrocella for a noble English captive,
Montferrers, and in the romantic tragedy of *Fortune by
Land and Sea*.

Heywood was also a fertile producer of non-dramatic
works. His poems include *Troia Britannica*, 1609, an
epic in nineteen cantos ; *The Life and Death of Hector*,
1614; various elegies and epithalamia ; and *The Hier-
archy of Angels*, not printed until 1635, in a handsome
folio with engraved plates. None of these have taken
any place in literature, but Heywood occasionally wrote
lyrics of great charm.

This is from the "true Roman tragedy" of *The Rape
of Lucrece*, published in 1609—

> Now, what is love I will thee tell,
> It is the fountain and the well
> Where pleasure and repentance dwell,
> It is, perhaps, the sancing bell
> That rings all in to heaven or hell ;
> And this is love, and this is love, as I hear tell.

> Now what is love I will you show,—
> A thing that creeps and cannot go ;
> A prize that passeth to and fro ;
> A thing for me, a thing for moe ;
> And he that proves shall find it so,
> And this is love, and this is love, sweet friend, I trow.

Heywood was not one of those poets on whom the gaze of all critics turns, as to a star whose beams lend themselves to infinite analysis; it is easy enough to divide the clear rays in his one pencil of light. He is a poet who will never, in future, want his friends, but who will scarcely claim one lover. It is not possible to be enthusiastic over the memory of a gossip so cheerful, garrulous, and superficial as this haunter of the Strand and the Exchange. He has a thousand entertaining things to tell us about the shops and the shop-girls; about the handsome young gallants, and the shocking way in which they waste their money; about the affectations of citizen fathers, and the tempers of citizen mothers. He is the most confirmed button-holer of our poetical acquaintance; and if he were only a little more monotonous, he would be universally voted a bore. Somehow or other, he has a little group of listeners always round him; it is not easy to drag one's self away till his stories are finished. His voice trembles as he tells us the strangest, saddest tale of how this or that poor girl came to shame and sorrow—of how such a noble gentleman, whom we must have often seen in the streets, lost all his estate, and died in want; and though there is nothing new in what he tells us, and though he hurries with characteristic timidity over every embarrassing or painful detail, we cannot help paying his loquacity the tribute of our laughter and our tears.

As an example of the blank verse of Heywood, a speech of Young Lionel in *The English Traveller* may be quoted—

.To what may young men best compare themselves?
Better to what, than to a house new-built?
The fabric strong, the chambers well contriv'd,
Polish'd within, without well beautified ;
When all that gaze upon the edifice
Do not alone commend the workman's craft,
But either make it their fair precedent
By which to build another, or, at least,
Wish there to inhabit.   Being set to sale,
In comes a slothful tenant, with a family
As lazy and debauch'd ; rough tempests rise,
Until the roof, which, by their idleness
Left unrepaired, the stormy showers beat in,
Rot the main posts and rafters, spoil the rooms,
Deface the ceilings, and in little space
Bring it to utter ruin, yet the fault
Not in the architector that first reared it,
But him that should repair it.   So it fares
With us young men.   We are those houses made,
Our parents raise these structures, the foundation
Laid in our infancy.

One of the latest to attract attention of all the Jacobean
dramatists was Thomas Middleton, to whom, however,
recent criticism assigns an ever-increasing prominence.
Neither Hazlitt nor Charles Lamb, although the latter
did Middleton the signal service of copious quotations,
was nearly so much struck by his powers as our latest
critics have been.   The reason, probably, was to be
found in Middleton's extreme inequality, or rather, perhaps, in the persistence with which he combined with
men of talent far inferior to his own.   He seems to have
had no ambition, and his best plays were all posthumously
published.   He attracted very little notice in his own
lifetime ; to Ben Jonson he was nothing but " a base
fellow."   His style was irregular and careless ; but no one

even in that age had a more indubitable gift of saying those " brave sublunary things " which stir the pulse. A very odd tradition of criticism was, that Middleton's genius was essentially unromantic. This came possibly from the exclusive study of his somewhat boisterous comedies, but more probably arose from his direct and penetrating diction, which was singularly remote from the pompous and bombastic tradition of Elizabethan tragedy.

Thomas Middleton was born in London about 1570. It is not probable that he began to write before 1600, for there is little doubt that the volume entitled *Microcynicon, Six Snarling Satyrs*, which has generally been attributed to him, was written by T. Muffet. In Middleton's very first play, we find him collaborating with the author with whom he was to be so closely associated throughout his career ; but as not Rowley only, but Massinger also, was a boy in 1600, the original texture of *The Old Law* was probably entirely Middleton's. The early career of this dramatist is peculiarly obscure. It is probable that two, or perhaps three, of his existing plays were written before the accession of James the First. The two comedies of *The Phœnix*, and *Michaelmas Term*, were probably acted very early in the reign, although they were not published until 1607. In the following year were printed *A Trick to Catch the Old One*, and *The Family of Love ;* the pro-logue of the second play modestly acknowledges the obscurity of the author, and the small favour that he has yet gained with the public. If Mr. Fleay is correct, all Middleton's plays up to this date had been written only for companies of boys. *A Match at Midnight*, and

A Mad World, my Masters, evidently belong to this early period.

As early as 1604, Middleton had been employed to help Dekker; but in 1613 we find him beginning to write these compositions on his own account, and presenting such figures as Envy " eating of a human heart, mounted on a Rhinoceros, attired in red silk, suitable to the bloodiness of her manners." Three plays, written by Middleton alone, are conjectured to belong to this period; they are *A Chaste Maid in Cheapside, No Wit Like a Woman's*, and the tragedy in which he first showed the full force of his genius, *Women beware Women*. About 1616 the regular partnership of Mid. dleton and Rowley seems to have commenced, and the first product of it was the spirited and original play, called *A Fair Quarrel*. At this point it becomes exceedingly difficult to form any plausible conjecture as to the relative dates of Middleton's and Rowley's plays, or to assign to either his proper share in their composition.

In 1620 Middleton was admitted to the office of City Chronologer, a post which he held until his death. It was apparently his duty to produce a sort of newspaper, which, however, was not to be printed. The manuscript of this chronicle was still in existence in the middle of the eighteenth century, but has since disappeared. The dramatic genius of Middleton had by this time advanced to its highest perfection, and we proceed to the enumeration of some very admirable works. In the group of romantic tragedies and tragi-comedies which he now began to produce, it is probable that *The Witch*, a tragedy not published until 1770, was the earliest in point of time, though certainly not the first in order of merit. The interesting relation of this drama to *Macbeth* has given a peculiar interest to *The Witch;* it is hardly necessary to say that Middleton's weird sisters are much later, not only than Shakespeare's, but than Ben Jonson's. There is, however, a curious doubt whether some of the songs now printed in *Macbeth* may not have been the composition of Middleton. Far superior in merit to *The Witch* are the magnificent plays of *The Changeling* and *The Spanish Gipsy*, the underplot of each of which may be attributed to Rowley.

In 1623 Middleton returned to his comedies, with *More Dissemblers besides Women* and *A Game at Chess*. When the latter play was acted in August, 1624, Gondemar, the Spanish ambassador, who had been satirized in it as the Black Knight, made a formal protest; the comedy was suppressed, and Middleton was thrown into prison. The list of Middleton's plays closes with the two comedies of *The Widow* and *Anything for a Quiet Life*, the dates of which, however, are quite uncertain. Middleton died in 1627, being buried on the 4th of July in the parish churchyard of Newington Butts.

The strength of Middleton lies, not in his rather gross and careless comedies, but in his romantic dramas, his singularly imaginative tragedies and tragi-comedies. Lamb, although he seems scarcely to have appreciated Middleton, speaks with extreme felicity of his " exquisiteness of moral sensibility, making one to gush out tears of delight." There is, unfortunately, too much of Middleton in existence ; a single volume might be selected which would give readers an exceedingly high impression of

his genius. He had no lyrical gift, and his verse, although
it is enlivened by a singularly brilliant and unexpected
diction, is not in itself of any great beauty. There is no
better example of Middleton's work, to which a student
can be recommended, than the serious part of *The
Changeling.* Mr. Bullen has spoken of the great scene
between De Flores and Beatrice as "unequalled outside
Shakespeare's greatest tragedies," and the praise can
hardly be held excessive. The plot of *The Changeling,*
which turns on the stratagem of a girl who, being in love
with one man, and affianced to a second, turns to a third
to extricate her from her difficulty, is in the highest
degree curious and novel. But when De Flores has
been persuaded to murder Alonzo, Beatrice is no nearer
to Alsemero ; for De Flores and his insolent conditions
stand in her way. At length she has to confess Alonzo's
murder to her lover, and the play ends, crudely, in a
cluster of deaths. But nothing in Jacobean drama is
finer than the desperate flutterings of Beatrice, or the
monstrous determination of De Flores.

Another great play of Middleton's is *The Spanish
Gipsy*, but this is of a far less gloomy type, although it
opens with menacing gravity. The air lightens as the
plot develops, and we assist at length at the denoûment
of a graceful and peaceful comedy, drawn on the combined lines of two stories from Cervantes. Some writers
have considered that the finest of Middleton's plays is the
tragedy of *Women beware Women*, but to admit this
would be to excuse too much what we may call the
ethical tastelessness of the age. The story of *Women
beware Women* is so excessively disagreeable, and the

play closes in a manner so odious, that the reader's sympathy is hopelessly alienated. This radical fault may perhaps disturb, but can scarcely destroy our appreciation of the beauty and invention of the style. The scene between Livia and the widow may be by Middleton or by Rowley; the polish and elasticity of the verse may probably induce us to conjecture the former. We have yet to mention, in analyzing Middleton's masterpieces, the passages which he contributed to *A Fair Quarrel.* The duel scene in which Captain Agar fights with his friend the colonel to avenge his mother's honour is the best-known existing page of Middleton, for Charles Lamb drew especial attention to it in his *Specimens.* That it is Middleton's can scarcely be questioned; all competent critics will agree with Mr. Bullen when he says, "to such a height of moral dignity and artistic excellence Rowley never attained."

The early comedies of Middleton are curiously incoherent in form; scarcely one but contains passages of high romantic beauty. Later on, his comic talent became more assured and less fitful, but the plays lose the Elizabethan flavour of romance; passages of pure poetry become rarer and rarer in them. It is very difficult to obtain any satisfaction out of such incongruous work as, for instance, *More Dissemblers besides Women.* On the other hand, *A Game of Chess,* which gained for Middleton more money and notoriety than all of his other works put together, is a patriotic comedy of real delicacy and distinction, and of all Middleton's non-tragic plays is probably the one which may be studied with most satisfaction by the modern reader. Popular

as political scandal made this play, it is yet almost
incredible that the receipts at its performance amounted
to fifteen hundred pounds, but if half of this is true, it
must have thrown a flush of real success over the close
of Middleton's laborious life.

The following speech of Isabella, in the tragedy
Woman beware Women, may serve as an example of the
style of Middleton—

<blockquote>
Marry a fool!
Can there be greater misery to a woman
That means to keep her days true to her husband,
And know no other man? so virtue wills it.
Why, how can I obey and honour him,
But I must needs commit idolatry?
A fool is but the image of a man,
And that but ill made neither.   O the heart-breakings
Of miserable maids where love's enforc'd!
The lost condition is but bad enough;
When women have their choices, commonly
They do but buy their thraldoms, bring great portions
To man to keep 'em in subjection;
As if a fearful prisoner should bribe
The keeper to be good to him, yet lies in still,
And glad of a good usage, a good look sometimes.
By'r lady, no misery surmounts a woman's;
Men buy their slaves, but women buy their masters;
Yet honesty and love makes all this happy,
And next to angels', the most blest estate.
That Providence, that has made every poison
Good for some use, and sets four warring elements
At peace in man, can make a harmony
In things that are most strange to human reason.
O but this marriage!
</blockquote>

It is exceedingly difficult to disengage Middleton from
his obscurer coadjutor William Rowley, who was probably

about fifteen years Middleton's junior. Rowley was writing for the stage as early as 1607, and continued to do so for twenty years. In 1637 he was married, in London, and we know absolutely nothing more about him. It is very doubtful at what moment the two friends began to collaborate, and we can first be certain of identifying their common work, when they join to produce *A Fair Quarrel* in 1617. Rowley had a small part in a great many subsequent dramas; but, for Middleton only, he seemed to have worked with regularity. In *The Birth of Merlin*, we have an unimportant tragi-comedy of Rowley's with which the name of Shakespeare was in some indefinable way associated. The well-known comedy of *The Maid of the Mill* was probably written by Rowley and Fletcher. But the first play, which we are able to trace, entirely written by Rowley, was *All's lost by Lust*, acted about 1622, and *A New Wonder, a Woman never vexed*, was also attributed to him alone. Each of Rowley's principal plays attracted the attention of Charles Lamb, who quotes largely from them. It is by these two works that Rowley must be judged, and in neither is his style seen to be of the first order. His tragedy is rough and coarse, founded upon the imitation of Middleton, but even more irregular in workmanship, and less brilliant in the critical passages. Yet I know not where we can be certain of observing the tragic style of Rowley, except in the crude and fierce pages of *All's lost by Lust*.

His gift in comedy can be more easily observed, and in particular *A New Wonder* is a typical instance of it. Even here, however, we feel that to be dogmatic

would be to be rash, and that Rowley holds, in existing
drama, such a subaltern position that it is very difficult
to form an opinion with regard to his talent. He is a
kitchen-maid rather than a cook, and it is impossible to
be certain what share he has had in the preparation of
any comic feast that is set before us. So far, however,
as we are able to form an opinion, we are apt to consider
that the influence of Rowley upon Middleton was an un-
wholesome one. Middleton was strangely compacted
of gold and clay, of the highest gifts and of the lowest
subterfuges of the playwright. In Rowley, all that was
not clay was iron, and it is difficult to believe that he
sympathized with or encouraged his friend's ethereal
eccentricities. That Rowley had a hand in the underplot of several of Middleton's noblest productions does
not alter our conviction that his own sentiments were
rather brutal and squalid, and that he cared for little but
to pander to the sensational instincts of the groundlings. The mutual attitude of these friends has been
compared to that of Beaumont and Fletcher, but it is
hard to think of Middleton in any other light than as
a poet unequally yoked with one whose temper was
essentially prosaic.

A very large number of plays were issued during the
first ten years of the century which were either written
by men who achieved no wide celebrity as dramatists,
or else cannot in the present condition of knowledge be
identified with any writer whatever. When we consider
that before the end of the reign of James I., something
like seven hundred plays had been published in England,
the fecundity of our early drama may seem positively

astonishing. It would be going too far to pretend that all of these plays displayed meritorious qualities ; but it is a very remarkable fact that almost every play of the period seems to possess some touch of vigorous vitality. The remainder of this chapter may be occupied with the enumeration of some of the most notable single plays of the early part of the reign. A very popular play was *Greene's Tu Quoque*, written by a man who lives in literature on the strength of a beautiful couplet of Mr. Swinburne's—

> Cooke, whose light boat of song one soft breath saves,
> Sighed from an amorous maiden's mouth of verse.

John (not Joseph) Cooke died in 1612, but his play was first printed in 1614.

It was the distinction of George Wilkins to have been associated with Shakespeare in the composition of *Pericles*, but Wilkins was also the author of an exceedingly popular drama, *The Miseries of Enforced Marriage*, first printed in 1607. Lodowick Barry was an Irish gentleman who produced in 1611 a boisterous comedy called *Ram Alley*, which long preserved its vogue. Edward Sharpham wrote *The Fleare* and *Cupid's Whirligig*, each in 1607. Samuel Rowley, of whom scarcely anything is known, may or may not have been an elder brother of Middleton's coadjutor. He seems to have been an actor as well as a playwright, and to have been regularly engaged in the latter capacity from 1599 until the end of James I.'s reign. None of his existing works call for separate mention. Gervaise Markham printed in 1608 *The Dumb Knight*, a romantic comedy founded upon a novel of Bandello. Markham was a very voluminous author of prose volumes. During the first year of James I.'s reign, it is supposed that Anthony Brewer produced his comedy of *The Country Girl*, and his tragedy of *The Love-sick King*, although these were not printed until half a century later. John Mason printed in 1610 a spirited, though roughly versified, tragedy of *The Turk*. Finally, to bring this tedious list to a close, two Smiths, Wentworth and William, who have been confounded with one another and with Shakespeare, were actively engaged in writing plays, most of which have disappeared. Of these the only one at all accessible is *The Hector of Germany*, by William Smith.

It now remains to describe three or four remarkable dramas which have hitherto eluded every species of investigation, and remain absolutely anonymous. In 1606 was printed the exceedingly lively and interesting comedy in verse, called *Nobody and Somebody*, to which attention was first directed by the German critic, Tieck. It presents us with such an entertaining picture of contemporary manners, that it is unfortunate that we cannot even conjecture by what apparently practised hand it was written; it was early translated into German. A great deal of conjectural criticism has been expended over the very fine play called *The Second Maiden's Tragedy*, but without resulting in any absolute certainty. Mr. Swinburne has strongly argued in favour of the claim of Chapman, and Mr. Fleay no less vigorously on behalf of Cyril Tourneur. The play, which was not printed until 1824, was composed in 1611, and was attributed to the actor Robert Gough, who is not known to have written anything. It is a very gloomy and violent piece of work, executed, however, with more than usual care, and very finely versified. The long-winded prose comedy of *Sir Giles Goosecap*, which was printed in 1606, has had its admirers; but a much more interesting dramatic work is *Swetnam, the Woman-hater, Arraigned by Women*, which was printed in 1620, and probably written a few years earlier. Joseph Swetnam was the author of a very savage prose attack on women, and the anonymous play formed an incident in the polemic that his book aroused. The plot was taken from a chivalrous Spanish novel of the time, and *Swetnam the Woman-hater* is remarkable for the unusually high moral tone it adopts with regard to women.

A very striking anonymous play is the comedy of *The Fair Maid of the Exchange*, published in 1607. It is a simple and straightforward sketch of London life at the opening of the 17th century, and is a favourable specimen of the class of cleanly comedy that promised to produce so much good work, and which was, unfortunately, soon spoiled by the passion for licentious intrigue to which Beaumont and Fletcher pandered so readily. Nothing can be brighter than the *mise en scène* of this play; we see the Royal Exchange (the Burlington Arcade of that day), full of smart shops, gay with passers and loungers, a little sunny centre of the business life of the City. Here the Cripple of Fenchurch Street has his stall, a tradesman, but wealthy, and heroic in mind and body; here Miss Phillis Flower, the unconscious cynosure of neighbouring eyes, lays out her lawns and satins before a loitering public of worshipping young gallants; here the fashionable young men come to strut

and lounge, and take liberties with the tradespeople
whose wealth they envy and whose purse-strings they are
glad to pull. The opening scene of the play, where
Phillis and Ursula are attacked at night by two ruffians
at Mile End, and are rescued by the clutch of the stout-
hearted cripple, and where the dastardly pair, returning
in the dark, knock the Cripple down, who in turn is
rescued by Frank Golding, is most happily devised, and
has the additional merit of introducing us at once to all
the principal characters. The Cripple is a delightful
creation ; but our interest in the plot falls off somewhat
when we discover that he refuses or dares not accept the
love that Phillis proffers him, and the notion of making
the tall and handsome Frank personate the Cripple so
perfectly as to deceive the girl who loves the latter, and
win away her heart, is incredible and unnatural. This
play is, however, noticeable for its very high tone of
feeling and complete originality of design.

A song which Frank Golding sings in *The Fair Maid
of the Exchange* may close the present chapter—

> Ye little birds that sit and sing
> Amidst the shady valleys,
> And see how Phillis sweetly walks
> Within her garden-alleys ;
> Go, pretty birds, about her bower !
> Sing, pretty birds, she may not lower !
> Ah me, methinks I see her frown !
> Ye pretty wantons warble.
>
> Go tell her through your chirping bills,
> As you by me are bidden,
> To her is only known my love,
> Which from the world is hidden ;

Go, pretty birds, and tell her so ;
See that your notes strain not too low,
For still methinks I see her frown,—
    Ye pretty wantons warble.

Go tune your voices' harmony,
And sing I am her Lover ;
Strain loud and sweet, that every note,
With sweet content may move her ;
And she that hath the sweetest voice,
Tell her I will not change my choice,
Yet still methinks I see her frown,—
    Ye pretty wantons warble.

O fly, make haste, see, see, she falls
Into a pretty slumber ;
Sing round about her rosy bed
That waking she may wonder ;
Say to her, 'tis her lover true,
That sendeth love to you, to you ;
And when you hear her kind reply,- -
Return with pleasant warblings.

CHAPTER VII.

GILES AND PHINEAS FLETCHER—BROWNE.

It is now time to discuss those non-dramatic writers who remained throughout the Jacobean period entirely devoted to the Spenserian tradition. Among these Giles Fletcher the younger was the most original and brilliant. He was a scion of that great house of poets to whom our early literature owed so much. His father, Giles the elder, was the Russian traveller and the author of *Licia;* his elder brother, Phineas, wrote *The Purple Island;* his cousin was John Fletcher, the dramatist. The exact date of his birth is unknown, but circumstances point to 1585 as the probable year. The death of Queen Elizabeth gave him his first opportunity of appearing before the public, in a *Canto upon the Death of Eliza,* which was printed at Cambridge in 1603. In many respects it is a remarkable little poem, especially as showing the lad to have been already intellectually and artistically adult. The form of stanza chosen is exactly what Giles selected afterwards for his epic; and what has never been used (with a doubtful exception to be presently mentioned) before or since by any one but himself.

The relation to Spenser, too, whose followers in style the whole family of the Fletchers distinctly were, is just as determined and scarcely more excessive than in his *Christ's Victory.* All that can be said is that the *Canto* displays none of those sudden intense beauties that are a wonder and a delight in its author's finished style.

Seven quiet years of clerical study at Cambridge preceded the publication of Giles Fletcher's second and only other book, which we shall proceed to examine. Its success was very small; the modest author put aside without a sigh the lyre that "malicious tongues" told him was out of tune; he became popular at Cambridge as a preacher for a little while, took then a living in a seaside hamlet of Suffolk, where the rough people mis-read his gentleness, and falling by degrees into melan-choly, he died soon, in 1623, being at the most not forty years of age. As a poet his career closed at twenty-five, earlier than Shelley's or Beaumont's. In spite of those "malicious tongues," the piety of his brother Phineas made his fame live just long enough at Cambridge to fire with imperishable fancies the young and ardent spirit of Milton.

Of all the works written in direct discipleship of Spenser, *Christ's Victory* is undoubtedly the most coherent and the best. Such prodigies as *Psyche* can only be reverenced far off; such masses of poetic concrete as *The Purple Island* were made to dip into and to quote from. *Christ's Victory* has the great advantage of being easy to read all through. In its style, again, we note a distinction between its author and the other learned and more or less admirable Spenserians; while their highest success was found in gaining for a iittle time that serene magnificence, without distinct elevation, which bore their model on upon so soft and so steady a wing, Giles Fletcher aimed at higher majesties of melody and imagination than Spenser attempted, and not unfrequently he reached a splendour of phrase for a parallel to which we search the *Faery Queen* in vain. At the same time, it must not, in all candour, be forgotten that he lived in an age of rapid poetic decadence, and that his beautiful fancies are sometimes obscured by an uncouth phraseology and a studied use of bizarre and tasteless imagery. These improprieties and extravagancies of form have, it cannot be denied, a certain whimsical charm of their own, like the romanesque ornaments of debased periods in Art, nor would it be necessary to dwell on them as a positive blemish, if their adoption in poetry had not so often been proved to be the inevitable precursor of decay. But these, after all is said, and their magnitude pressed to its full, are slight stains on a writer otherwise so royally robed in pure poetic purple.

Christ's Victory and Triumph is the first important religious poem in seventeenth-century English. The full title is *Christ's Victory and Triumph in Heaven and Earth, Over and After Death,* and it is divided into four books, characterized by these four divisions of the epical theme. The stanza in which it is written is the nine-lined one of Spenser, compressed into an octett by the omission of the seventh line, and so deprived of that fourth rhyme which is one of its greatest technical difficulties. When it is added that each book contains from sixty to eighty of these stanzas, it will be perceived on how moderate and reserved a scale the whole has been composed; and the treatment is sensibly rendered more impressive by this very reserve. "Christ's Victory in Heaven" begins with a long array of theological paradoxes in the favourite manner of the time, but expressed with exceptional dignity; we soon find ourselves taken up to heaven and made present at that precise moment of the past ages in which Mercy—

> Lift up the music of her voice, to bar
> Eternal Fate, lest it should quite erase
> That from the world which was the first world's grace.

Justice, however, rises to oppose her, and on this impersonation Fletcher has poured out the richest treasures of his imagination. In a strain that recalls the ripest manner of Keats, the manner that is of *Hyperion* and the last sonnets, he cries—

> She was a Virgin of austere regard;
>   Not as the world esteems her, deaf and blind;
> But as the eagle that hath oft compared
>   Her eye with Heaven's, so, and more brightly shined
>   Her lamping sight.

A little later on and we might persuade ourselves that it was Shelley speaking, and in *Adonaïs*—

> The wingèd lightning is her Mercury,
>   And round about her mighty thunders sound;
> Impatient of himself lies pining by
>   Pale Sickness with his kercher'd head upwound.

The argument of Justice being that mankind has sinned so grossly against its Maker that it is now beyond

the pale of hope, Mercy rises to defend the fallen against
so sweeping a denunciation. The description of her
personality might have served Coleridge with a text for
his favourite sermon on the difference between imagination and fancy. Great is the falling off from the simple
grandeur of the picture of Justice; the charm here is
more superficial, the language more affected. Mercy is
robed in garments by herself embroidered with trees and
towers, beasts, and all the wonders of the world. Above
her head she wears a headdress of azure crape, held up
by silver wire, in which golden stars are burning against
a flood of milk-white linen; a diamond canopy hangs
over her, supported by little dancing angels and by King
David. After she has pleaded, Repentance rises, dis-
consolate and ill-favoured, with her hair full of ashes,
whom Mercy pauses to comfort—

> Such when as Mercy her beheld from high,
>   In a dark valley, drowned with her own tears,
> One of her Graces she sent hastily,
>   Smiling Irene, that a garland wears
>   Of gilded olive on her fairer hairs,
> To crown the fainting soul's true sacrifice;
>   Whom when as sad Repentance coming spies,
> The holy desperado wiped her swollen eyes.

Mercy at once comforting Repentance and assuaging
Justice, charges the worst of Man's fault upon the Devil,
and celebrates Christ from his nativity. The book closes
so, with a peroration that is sometimes strangely Miltonic,
as in these lines—

> The angels carolled loud their song of praise,
>   The cursed oracles were stricken dumb,

which Milton simply transferred to his *Ode on the Morning of Christ's Nativity.*

The second part, "Christ's Victory on Earth," is inferior in purity of style to the preceding. It is much more overloaded with figurative language of a rococo kind, with a choice of imagery which sacrifices propriety to magnificence, and with that paradoxical kind of ornament which is called conceit. Mercy, in her coach, attended by a thousand loves, finds Christ in the wilderness, and sinks, unperceived, into His breast. He is then minutely described in pretty and even luxurious language, which resembles nothing so much as the jewelled pictures of Fra Lippo Lippi and Benozzo Gozzoli, full of flowers and tall plants, gems and rare raiment, and angels with brilliant wings, where all is sumptuous, but the face of the Madonna meaningless and vapid. So the description here of Christ, with his curly jet hair and his strawberry-cream complexion, is too pretty to be in keeping with the solemnity of the subject. Soon we come to the most famous stanza in the whole poem—

> At length an aged sire far off he saw,
>   Came slowly footing ; every step he guessed.
> One of his feet he from the grave did draw ;
>   Three legs he had—the wooden was the best ;
>   And all the way he went, he ever blest
> With benedicites and prayérs' store ;
> But the bad ground was blesséd n'er the more ;
> And all his head with snow of age was waxen hoar.

> A good old hermit he might seem to be,
>   That for devotion had the world forsaken,
> And now was travelling some saint to see,
>   Since to his beads he had himself betaken,
>   Where all his former sins he might awaken,

> And then might rush away with dropping brine,
> And alms, and fasts, and church's discipline,
> And, dead, might rest his bones under the holy shrine.

This, it will be remembered, Milton made good use of in *Paradise Regained*, which should be read all through in connection with Giles Fletcher's poem.   Fletcher, in his turn, is here specially under obligation to Spenser, from whom we find him presently borrowing two whole lines. The most significant passage in the rest of this canto is the description of the garden and the court of Vain-Glory, in which Fletcher attempts the peculiar style of which Spenser is most admirably a master, and approaches with extraordinary success to the sumptuous and splendid richness of his original.

The two remaining cantos are not so easy to describe, though none the less beautiful.   " Christ's Triumph over Death " is a philosophical disquisition on the various modes in which the universe was affected by the Triumph ; there is now no action and little description.   We read here of the crucifixion, with the shame of earth and the anger of heaven, where—

> The mazèd angels shook their fiery wings,
> Ready to lighten vengeance from God's Throne,

and of Christ's earlier passion in the garden.   The fourth canto, " Christ's Triumph after Death," is, in fact, an ecstatic hymn of the Resurrection, and the beatific vision of God in Paradise.   The gorgeous and luminous style of Giles Fletcher here reaches its highest pitch, and we find ourselves reminded, though without imitation, of Dante's *Paradiso.*   The joys of heaven and earth in

redemption are celebrated with a splendour of language
hardly to be met with elsewhere in the whole of Protestant
religious literature.

> It is no flaming lustre, made of light ;
>   No sweet concent or well-tim'd harmony ;
> Ambrosia, for to feast the appetite,
>   Or flowery odour mix'd with spicery ;
>   No soft embrace, or pleasure bodily ;
> And yet it is a kind of inward feast,
> A harmony, that sends within the breast
> An odour, light, embrace, in which the soul doth rest.
>
> A heavenly feast, no hunger can consume ;
>   A light unseen, yet shines in every place ;
> A sound, no time can steal ; a sweet perfume,
>   No winds can scatter ; an entire embrace,
>   That no satiety can e'er unlace ;
> Ingrac'd into so high a favour, there
> The saints with their beau-peres whole worlds outwear,
> And things unseen do see, and things unheard do hear.
>
> Ye blessèd souls, grown richer by your spoil,
>   Whose loss, though great, is cause of greater gains,
> Here may your weary spirits rest from toil,
>   Spending your endless evening, that remains,
>   Among those white flocks and celestial trains,
> That feed upon their Shepherd's eyes, and frame
> That heavenly music of so wondrous fame,
> Psalming aloud the holy honours of his name.

Between Giles Fletcher and his elder brother Phineas
there existed the closest fraternal affection and intellectual sympathy, and we find repeated in the works
of each identical fragments of expression. The difference
between them simply consisted in that indefinable
distinction between genius and talent. But while Giles

is for ever startling us with such incomparably poetic
phrases as "a globe of wingèd angels," "the laughing
blooms of sallow," "wide-flaming primroses," or "the
moon's burning horns," Phineas, who was not less
accomplished, and who lived to be far more voluminous,
never reaches this white heat of imagination. He is
none the less a poet of remarkable force and variety,
curiously individual, and worthy of close examination.
Phineas Fletcher was born at Cranbrook early in 1582,
the eldest son of Giles Fletcher the elder. He proceeded to Eton and to King's College, Cambridge,
residing at the University from 1600 to 1616. During
these years his poetry was mainly, if not entirely, written,
although most of it first saw the light far later; in 1611
he took priest's orders. In 1621 Phineas was presented
to the living of Hilgay in Norfolk, where he seems to
have stayed till the Civil War. In 1670 we are told that
he died "several years since;" many of his descendants
are said to exist still in the parish of Hilgay.

None of Phineas Fletcher's books were published
until after the reign of James I. But what was probably
the latest of them, the *Locustes*, appeared in 1627, the
"piscatory" play of *Sicelides* (written in 1614) in 1631,
and the volume containing *The Purple Island, or the
Isle of Man, together with Piscatory Eclogues and other
Poetical Miscellanies*, in 1633. The volume called the
Locustes contains the satire so named, which is in Latin
verse, and a paraphrase or poem of like theme in
English, composed in a nine-line stanza which closely
resembles the Spenserian. This is called *The Apollyonists*,
and it is a noble epic fragment on the Fall of the Rebel

Angels, with the figure of Satan as that of the hero ; a bitter attack on the Jesuits is introduced. Milton was not only well acquainted with the writings of Phineas Fletcher, but he paid to the *Apollyonists* the compliment of borrowing more from it than from any other work when he came to write his own *Paradise Lost. Sicelides* is a choral drama, principally in rhyme, with comic prose passages ; the romantic story, laid in Sicily, mainly pieced together with reminiscences from Ovid's *Metamorphoses.* The *Piscatory Eclogues* and the miscellaneous poems are so obviously variants in the manner of Phineas Fletcher's longest and most famous work that we may pass on without further delay to a description of the latter.

Successive generations of poetic readers have been disappointed to find that *The Purple Island* is not some purpureal province of fairyland washed by "perilous seas forlorn," but the ruddy body of man, laced with veins of purple blood. The poem, in fact, is an allegory descriptive of the corporeal and moral qualities of a human being, carried out with extreme persistence, even where the imagery is most grotesque and inconvenient. From internal indications, we may gather that *The Purple Island* was written early in Fletcher's Cambridge career, perhaps about 1605, while his brother was still at his side, and other ardent young spirits were stirring Phineas to literary emulation. When we recover from the first shock of the plan, we have to confess *The Purple Island* to be extremely ingenious, cleverly sustained, and adorned as tastefully as such an unseemly theme can be by the embroideries of imaginative writing. In mere

cleverness, few English poems of the same length have
excelled it, and its vivacity is sustained to the last
stanza of the last canto.

The poet supposes himself seated in summer under
the orchard walls of Cambridge, by the slow waters of
"learned Chamus," in company with two pleasant friends.
With them he discusses poetry, history, fate, and his own
biography, till the first canto closes with the announce-
ment that he proposes to sing the story of "the little
Isle of Man, or Purple Island." At the opening of the
second canto, Thirsil, for so he calls himself, is discovered
at sunset on a gentle eminence with "a lovely crew of
nymphs and shepherd boys" clustered around him, and
to this audience he pipes his strange anatomical ditty,
each successive canto, however grisly its theme, being
presented to us in a recurrence of this delicate pastoral
setting.

In canto two, we read of the foundation of the Purple
Island, its rescue from decay, the marble congelation
of its bones, the azure river-system of its veins and
arteries, the rose-white wall of its skin, and all the quaint
devices by which the poet idealizes its digestive system.
The third canto, after so exquisite an opening as this—

> The morning fresh, dappling her horse with roses,
>   Vexed at the lingering shades, that long had left her
> In Tithon's freezing arms, the light discloses,
>   And, chasing night, of rule and heaven bereft her,
> The sun with gentle beams his rage disguises,
>   And, like aspiring tyrants, temporises,
> Never to be endured, but when he falls or rises,

takes an immediate plunge into the liver and that

"porphyry house" in which "the Isle's great Steward,"
the heart, dwells. With all the humours and exudations
of the body Phineas Fletcher laboriously sports, with
a plentiful show of such physiology as was then attainable.
In canto four the heart again and the lungs are treated ;
in canto five the head, the face, and the organs which
occur in it. After describing the tongue, the story of
Eurydice is told, and the anatomical portion of the
allegory is concluded.

It is a pity that the physiology presses in so early in
the poem, for the most beautiful part is yet to come.
With canto six, the intellectual and moral qualities pass
under consideration, and in particular we are introduced
to the will, as fair Voletta, and to that "royal damsel and
faithful counsellor" Synteresis, the conscience. In cantos
seven and eight, the vices are personified at great length
and with remarkable vigour ; in cantos nine and ten,
the virtues are similarly introduced. Cantos eleven and
twelve describe a sort of holy war in Man's members,
and the battle between virtue and vice which revolution-
izes the Purple Island.   Such is the rough outline of
a work which resembles none other in our language, and
which is so curious and interesting in its workmanship as
to forbid us to lament the extraordinary nature of the
author's original plan. Having chosen a theme of unusual ugliness and aridity, Phineas Fletcher has contrived
so to treat it as to produce a work of positive, though of
course Alexandrine and fantastic beauty.

A passage describing the shepherd's life may be quoted
as an example of the more poetic texture of *The Purple
Island*—

His certain life, that never can deceive him,
  Is full of thousand sweets and rich content ;
The smooth-leaved beeches in the field receive him
  With coolest shades, till noon-tide's rage is spent ;
His life is neither tossed in boisterous seas
Of troublous world, nor lost in slothful ease ;
Pleased and full blessed he lives, when he his God can please.

His bed of wool yields safe and quiet sleep,
  While by his side his faithful spouse hath place ;
His little son into his bosom creeps,
  The lively picture of his father's face ;
Never his humble house or state torment him ;
Less he could like, if less his God had sent him,
And when he dies, green turf with grassy tomb content him.

The relation of Phineas Fletcher to Spenser is very
close, but the former possesses a distinct individuality.
He is enamoured to excess of the art of personification,
and the allegorical figures he creates in so great abundance
are distinct and coherent, with, as a rule, more of Sackville than of Spenser in the evolution of their types.   In
his eclogues he imitates Sannazaro, but not without a
reminiscence of *The Shepherd's Calendar.*   Nevertheless,
Spenser is the very head and fount of his being, and the
source of some of his worst mistakes, for so bound is
Phineas to the Spenserian tradition that he clings to it
even where it is manifestly unfitted to the subject he has
in hand.

In 1628 there was published a small poem called
Britain's Ida, attributed by the publisher to "that
renowned poet Edmund Spenser." It is obvious that
Spenser did not write this elaborate and highly Jacobean
piece of voluptuousness, which bears the stamp of *circa*

1608. There is absolutely no rumour identifying *Britain's Ida*, which shows the influence of Shakespeare almost as strongly as that of Spenser, with any name. But it is composed in the very peculiar stanza invented by Giles Fletcher, and it is full of phrases and locutions afterwards published in the writings of Phineas, who admits that before he indited the *Purple Island*, he had learned—

> in private shades to feign,
> Soft sighs of love unto a looser strain.

The use of double rhymes, what Mr. Saintsbury (in another connection) describes as "the adjustment of the harmony of the individual stanza as a verse paragraph," and the luscious picturesqueness of the imagery, irresistably suggest the Fletchers, neither of whom, in his youth, need have been ashamed of the workmanship of *Britain's Ida*, though to each of them its sensuality must in advanced years have seemed reprehensible. It is to be noted that Giles was dead, and Phineas still living, when this work was published, which gives some probability to the authorship of the former. *Britain's Ida*, an octavo pamphlet of nineteen leaves, is a narrative of the class of *Venus and Adonis*, in six brief cantos.

The song which the Boy hears proceeding from the bower in the Garden of Delight may be taken as a specimen of this melodious and sensuous poem :—

> Fond man, whose wretched care the life soon ending,
>   By striving to increase your joy, do end it ;
> And spending joy, yet find no joy in spending ;
>   You hurt your life by striving to amend it ;
>   Then, while fit time affords thee time and leisure,
>   Enjoy while yet thou may'st thy life's sweet pleasure ;
> Too foolish is the man that starves to feed his treasure.

> Love is life's end ; an end, but never ending ;
>   All joys, all sweets, all happiness, awarding ;
> Love is life's wealth ; ne'er spent, but ever spending ;
>   More rich by giving, taking by discarding ;
>   Love's life's reward, rewarded in rewarding ;
> Then from thy wretched heart fond care remove ;
> Ah ! should'st thou live but once love's sweet to prove,
> Thou wilt not love to live, unless thou live to love.

Yet another poetical Fletcher, and he also a clergy-man, was the rector of Wilby in Suffolk. It is, however, believed that Joseph Fletcher was not of the many-laurelled family. He was born about 1577, and from 1609 till his death in 1637 held the benefice above named. He seems to have written love-poems in his early career, "sweet baits to poison youth," (can it be he who wrote *Britain's Ida ?*) but these are lost. His existing works are two long High-Church devotional poems, *Christ's Bloody Sweat*, 1613, in six-line stanza, *The Perfect - Cursed - Blessed Man*, 1629, in heroic couplet. The latter is a ragged performance ; the former has a good deal of limpid Spenserian grace. A single stanza may give an idea of Joseph Fletcher's manner—

> He died, indeed, not as an actor dies,
>   To die to-day and live again to-morrow,
> In show to please the audience, or disguise
>   The idle habit of enforcèd sorrow ;
>   The cross his stage was, and he played the part
> Of one that for his friend did pawn his heart.

William Browne, of Tavistock, was born in 1588. He went to Exeter College, Oxford, about 1605, and thence to London, where he was admitted of the Inner Temple early in 1613. His first book of *Britannia's Pastorals* is addressed from that society a few months later, and, although the folio is undated, was probably issued at the close of 1613. An *Elegy* on Prince Henry was published in 1613, and *The Shepherd's Pipe* in 1614. *Book II.* of *Britannia's Pastorals* appeared in 1616; *Book III.*, which was preserved in manuscript in the Cathedral Library, Salisbury, not until 1851. The *Inner Temple Masque* was first printed, from the manuscript in Emmanuel College, Cambridge, in 1772, and his miscellaneous poems in 1815, so that all that was not posthumous of Browne's appeared before he was thirty. He went back to residence in Oxford in 1624, and is supposed to be the William Browne who was buried at Tavistock on the 27th of March, 1643. He was early the friend of Ben Jonson, Selden, and Drayton, but as life advanced grew melancholy and unsocial. Prince says that he had "a great mind in a little body."

The very high praise awarded by some critics to the poetry of Browne is somewhat unaccountable. To compare him with Keats, as has been done, is quite preposterous. In his work we have a return to the pure Elizabethan manner, loose and fluid versification, and ingenuous pursuit of simple beauty. But the early freshness of the pastoral poets is gone, and the archaic words, introduced in imitation of Spenser, have lost their illusion. Browne is happiest in single lines, such as—

> An uncouth place fit for an uncouth mind,

or,

> Shrill as a thrush upon a morn of May,

but these beauties are infrequent. His genuine love of natural scenery and phenomena gives charm to his

occasional episodes, and his poems have a species of
local propriety; they suggest his early haunts, the Tavy
brawling down from Dartmoor between its rocks and
wooded glens, the ancient borough of Tavistock, the
" sandy Plim," and, farther away, the Channel with its
" sea-binding chains." Vaguely, and at intervals, this
Devonshire scenery is revealed to us for a moment by a
turn in Browne's conventional poetry.

A sort of story runs through the long, unfinished poem
in heroic couplet called *Britannia's Pastorals*, but it is
exceedingly difficult to seize. The first book was
published in 1613, the same year that saw the issue of
the *Poly-Olbion*, but Browne sings of " dear Britannia"
in a mode diametrically opposed to that of his friend
Drayton. There is neither geography, nor antiquity,
nor, in spite of a flourish about

The snow-white cliffs of fertile Albion,

even patriotism. It is simply a very vague and mawkish
tale of semi-supernatural love-making in south-western
Devonshire. There is one Marina, who, loving Celandine,
but doubtful of the direction of his passion, determines
on suicide in the Tavy. She flings herself in, and a
young shepherd takes her out again. The story moves
at a snail's pace, amid unrestrained long-winded dialogue.
Marina, still despairing, flings herself into a well or pool,
and the first canto closes. The God of the pool saves
her, and he and a nymph, his sister, converse, at extreme
length, in octosyllabics. Marina casually drinks of a
magic spring, and has the good fortune to forget
Celandine. But a wicked shepherd carries her off in

a boat. It is hardly necessary to follow the thread of narrative further, for Browne was absolutely devoid of all epic or dramatic talent. His maids and shepherds have none of the sweet plausibility which enlivens the long recitals of Spenser. They outrage all canons of common sense. When a distracted mother wants to know if a man has seen her lost child, she makes the inquiry in nineteen lines of deliberate poetry. An air of silliness broods over the whole conception. Marina meets a lovely shepherd, whose snowy buskins display a still silkier leg, and she asks of him her way to the marish; he misunderstands her to say "marriage," and tells her that the way is through love; she misunderstands him to refer to some village so entitled, and the languid comedy of errors winds on through pages.

The best of the poem consists in its close and pretty pictures of country scenes. At his best, Browne is a sort of Bewick, and provides us with vignettes of the squirrel at play, a group of wrens, truant schoolboys, or a country girl,

> When she upon her breast, love's sweet repose,
> Doth bring the Queen of Flowers, the English Rose.

But these happy "bits" are set in a terrible waste of what is not prose, but poetry and water, foolish babbling about altars and anagrams, long lists of blooms and trees and birds, scarcely characterized at all, soft rhyming verse meandering about in a vaguely pretty fashion to no obvious purpose. On the first book of *Britannia's Pastorals* the stamp of extreme youth is visible clearly enough; but the second book, which belongs to Browne's manhood, and the two cantos of the third, which probably date from his advanced age, show little more skill in the evolution of a story, or power in making the parts of a poem mutually cohere.

The seven eclogues of the *Shepherd's Pipe* which are Browne's (for this was a composite work in which Brooke, Wither, and Davies of Hereford joined) are designed closely in the manner of Spenser, in lyrical measures of great variety and not a little sweetness. The fourth, on the death of Philarete, is the finest, and is supposed to have influenced Milton in the composition of *Lycidas;* for this is an elegy, rather than an eclogue, and a very melodious specimen of its class. It may be interesting to note, as showing the especial attraction felt by Milton to all the poets of this Spenserian school, that in Mr. Huth's library there exists a copy of Browne copiously annotated in the hand of his great successor. The *Inner Temple Masque*, which was prepared for performance about 1617, opens with this Song of the Sirens, the most perfect of Browne's poems—

> Steer hither, steer your wingèd pines,
>   All beaten mariners !
> Here lie love's undiscovered mines,
>   A prey to passengers,—
> Perfumes far sweeter than the best
> Which make the Phœnix' urn and nest ;
>   Fear not your ships,
> Nor any to oppose you save our lips ;
>   But come on shore,
> Where no joy dies till love hath gotten more.
>
> For swelling waves, our panting breasts,
>   Where never storms arise,
> Exchange ; and be awhile our guests,
>   For stars gaze in our eyes ;

> The compass Love shall hourly sing,
> And as he goes about the ring,
>   We will not miss
> To tell each point he nameth with a kiss ;
>   Then come on shore,
> Where no joy dies till love hath gotten more.

The masque, a slight and picturesque affair, deals with the story of Circe and Ulysses. Among the miscellaneous poems of Browne, now appears the celebrated epitaph on the Countess Dowager of Pembroke, long attributed to Ben Jonson—

> Underneath this sable hearse
> Lies the subject of all verse,
> Sidney's sister, Pembroke's mother ;
> Death, ere thou hast slain another
> Fair and learn'd and good as she,
> Time shall throw a dart at thee,

but the manner does not recall that of Browne, and the authorship of this pathetic trifle must still be held dubious.

A writer of the same class and group as Browne, but of inferior talent, has been revealed to us this year, and for the first time, by the piety of Mr. Warwick Bond. William Basse was born about 1583 and died about 1660. He published one or two pamphlets in the last years of Elizabeth, but after 1602 was scarcely heard of, although he wrote ambitiously and abundantly. Basse was the author of an elegy on Shakespeare, which was the only fragment of his writings familiar to any one until Mr. Bond edited his manuscript works. We may now study his *Pastorals*, his *Urania*, his *Metamorphosis of the Walnut-Tree*, and portions of his lost *Polyhymnia*. But

Basse, though an elaborate is a very tame and tedious rhymer, whose vein of Spenserian richness soon wore out, and left nothing but an awkward and voluble affectation behind it. He held a dependent position in the neighbourhood of Thame Park, and describes himself as one

> that ne'er gazed on Cheapside's glistening row,
> Nor went to bed by the deep sound of Bow,
> But lent my days to silver-colour'd sheep,
> And from strawn cotes borrowed my golden sleep.

Christopher Brooke retains a minute niche in literary history as the intimate friend of Donne and Browne, and as a singularly sympathetic companion of poets. Much was expected of him; in 1616 Browne declared of Brooke that his

> polished lines
> Are fittest to accomplish high designs,

but, beyond an occasional elegy or eclogue, he did nothing. Brooke was the " Cuttie" of the coterie who published *The Shepherd's Pipe*, to which he contributed a poem of small importance. He was the chamber-fellow to Donne, and shared the penalties of that passionate youth's clandestine marriage. Christopher Brooke is, among the Jacobean poets, the figure which every literary "set" supplies, the man in whom contemporary eyes detect endless promise of genius, and in whom posterity can see scarcely anything to arrest attention.

The age of James I. was not, like that of Elizabeth, rich in great poetical translators. Almost the only version which calls for notice is that of Lucan's *Phar-*

salia, by Sir Arthur Gorges, who died in 1625. Gorges, the kinsman of Sir Walter Raleigh, and the friend and associate of Spenser, was rather an Elizabethan than a member of our period. But he exchanged arms for poetry late in life, and did not produce his Lucan until 1614.

CHAPTER VIII.

A MAJESTIC but shadowy figure is rather conjectured than seen to cross the stage in the person of the author of *The Revenger's Tragedy*. Of no poet do we know less, and of none would it be more hazardous to conceive the way in which he moved and lived among his fellow-creatures. He may have been harmless and industrious, but if he can be supposed to be painted in his writings, he must have been the most caustic, insolent, and sinister of men. It is difficult to justify the fascination which the tragedies of Cyril Tourneur exercise over us. Works more faulty in construction, more inadequate in execution, more strained or hysterical in emotion can scarcely be found in the range of recognized dramatic literature. Those of us who have shaken with inward laughter over Voltaire's grave analysis of *Hamlet* and *le tendre Otway* cannot but feel how exquisitely funny, how preposterously monstrous, *The Atheist's Tragedy* would have seemed to the strong intelligence of the apostle of common sense. Indeed, to subject the writings of Tourneur to parody or burlesque would be a sheer waste of ingenuity. No transpontine melodrama could possibly, in its wildest flights of frenzy, approach the last act of *The Revenger;* no parodist in any happy moment of genius could hope to surpass the brilliant idea that induces Charlmont and Castabella, in the midst of an interesting churchyard conversation, suddenly to lie down in a grave, "with either of them a death's head for a pillow."

But in breathing the intense and magnetic air of Jacobean tragedy the purely modern notion of the ridiculous must be avoided as an explosive substance dangerous to the entire fabric of the imagination, and to laugh is to stir the thunder which may bring the whole house about our ears. Yet even when we approach Cyril Tourneur with chastened senses, and judge him by the standard of his contemporaries, we do not at once perceive the unique quality of his writing. It is hardly possible to compare the plays of Webster with those under consideration without perceiving that the author of *The Duchess of Malfy* was the superior in everything that appeals to the heart and the fancy, in tragic tenderness, in grasp of human character, in that flowery lyricism that robs death of half its horrors. Comparing Tourneur, again, with Ford, we must at once concede supremacy in passion and feeling to the later poet; and at last, by indulging thus in mere parallelisms, we may easily satisfy ourselves that Tourneur was a very indifferent poet indeed. And yet we read his two tragedies again and again; we are powerless to resist the spell of his barbaric harmonies, and we are forced to admit that he knew, in spite of all his crude affectations, the right mode to purge the soul with pity and terror.

Perhaps the best way to understand wherein the unique poetic element in Tourneur's work really consists is to read his greatest poem, *The Revenger's Tragedy*, once more carefully through. The opening impresses the imagination, but with some confusion. It is not wholly plain at first that Vindici stands on a balcony, with the skull of his mistress in his hand, and apostrophizes the wild throng of revellers who pass along the stage below by torchlight. This is weird and splendid in conception; but we pass on. Vindici has a brother Hippolito—a little tamer than himself—a mother, and a fair sister, Castiza. The poet desires to give the impression of a like unbending temper in each of the three children; he scarcely avoids making all three repulsive. We are presently introduced to a duke and duchess, and to their various children, five in number, whose figures pass in and out, engaged in more or less terrible vices, but almost undistinguishable to us who have no clue of face or dress to guide us.

The first act is concluded, and the peculiar power of the poet has not been revealed; but the second opens with a scene that rivets our attention. Vindici, in disguise, acts as pander between one of the Duke's sons and his own sister, Castiza, all the while earnestly trusting that she will resist his subtle arguments. His mother he seduces to connivance, or more; but Castiza has the stubborn virtue of her race. With much that is fantastic, it must be admitted that this situation is highly dramatic; but we are not deeply moved by it until the perverted mother attempts to over-persuade her daughter, and then we are lifted on a wave of excitement which breaks in something like agony as Castiza cries—

" Mother, come from that poisonous woman there."

This line, the finest in all Tourneur's writings, is the key-note to the charm he exercises over us in spite of our reason.   This fiery indignation ; this fierce severance of the sinner from the sin ; in short, the intense moral and intellectual sincerity underlying the jargon of an affected and imperfect style, and burning its way through into faultless expression at moments of the highest excitement—this is what fascinates and overpowers us in Cyril Tourneur.   He is as foul as Marston, but he loathes the filth he touches ; there is no amorous dandling of a beloved error as in Ford.   So patent is the sincerity of this man that we might even without paradox say that we value him more for what we feel he could have written than for anything he actually did write.   That his point of view is unhealthy ; that his knowledge of the heart was limited ; and that his lurid imagination dwelt only on the diseases of society, must not blind us to this sterling quality.

Our knowledge of Cyril Tourneur's life is entirely confined to the titles and dates of his works.   In 1600 he published a crude and affected poem in rime royal, called *The Transformed Metamorphosis*, which is as nearly worthless as possible.   *The Revenger's Tragedy*, which has been described above, was printed in 1607. In 1611 appeared *The Atheist's Tragedy*, which it has been usual to take for granted must have been written at a date precedent to 1607, because of its marked inferiority to the *Revenger ;* but this is a very unsafe argument, as the indubitably dated works of such writers as Dekker may suggest.   In 1612 Cyril Tourneur entered on the Stationer's Registers a tragi-comedy of

The Nobleman, which, to the great regret of his admirers, has disappeared. The same fate has overtaken *The Arraignement of London*, which was written in 1613 by Tourneur in combination with Daborne. When we have mentioned two short copies of verses, we have chronicled all that is known of Cyril Tourneur.

A very raw production, it must be confessed, is *The Atheist's Tragedy*, but it contains some magnificent passages of poetry. Among them the following is, or should be, known to every educated reader—

> Walking next day upon the fatal shore,
> Among the slaughtered bodies of their men,
> Which the full-stomach'd sea had cast upon
> The sands, it was my unhappy chance to light
> Upon a face, whose favour when it liv'd,
> My astonish'd mind inform'd me I had seen.
> He lay in his armour, as if that had been
> His coffin; and the weeping sea, like one
> Whose milder temper doth lament the death
> Of him whom in his rage he slew, runs up
> The shore, embraces him, kisses his cheek,
> Goes back again, and forces up the sands
> To bury him, and every time it parts
> Sheds tears upon him, till at last (as if
> It could no longer endure to see the man
> Whom it had slain, yet loath to leave him) with
> A kind of unresolv'd unwilling face,
> Winding her waves one in another, like
> A man that folds his arms or wrings his hands
> For grief, ebbed from the body, and descends
> As if it would sink down into the earth,
> And hide itself for shame of such a deed.

But Tourneur is quite unable to remain at this altitude of style. No themes appeal to him except those involved in gloom and horror, and this strict limitation of interests makes him fail, beyond the wont of his violent compeers, in dramatic propriety. Mr. Swinburne has happily said of *The Atheist's Tragedy* that "there never was such a thunderstorm of a play," so violent and black is the cloud that hangs over it, so fitful and lurid the occasional gleams of light. D'Amville, the bad hero of the play, is a murderous villain of the most incredible kind, whose only pleasure is to conspire against virtuous victims in a manner as crazy as it is atrocious. His generous son, Sebastian, scarcely relieves the blackness of the study. There is a vague charm about the lovers, Charlamont and Castabella. The versification, which one critic finds "rich, soft, and buoyant," to readers of ordinary senses will probably seem as harsh and inelastic, though certainly not as poor, as any they will meet with in the repertory of any indubitable poet. Certain passages always excepted, *The Atheist's Tragedy* would scarcely be read, were it not written by the author of *The Revenger's Tragedy*, which, with all its palpable short-comings, is one of the noblest productions of its class and time.

Among all the purely Jacobean dramatists there is not one who has drawn to himself so keen an interest from the poets and critics of the present century as John Webster, to whose work the transition from *The Revenger's Tragedy* is unusually easy. It is unfortunate that so singular and sympathetic a figure should be to us a name and hardly anything more. He was probably born about 1580, and he tells us that he was "one born free of the Merchant-Tailors' Company." According to Gildon— who wrote, it is true, nearly a century later—he was clerk of St. Andrew's Parish in Holborn. He made his will, and probably died, in 1625. He began to write for the stage about 1602, and was originally one of those collaborators who were so numerous at that period, and are now so perplexing to critics. We need not, perhaps, regret that *Cæsar's Fall* and *Two Harpies*, which he produced in company with Drayton and others in 1602, are lost, suggestive as is the second title. In 1607 was published *The Famous History of Sir Thomas Wyatt*, which is considered to be Webster's and Dekker's portion of a composite play written by them and three others in the year 1602. The conditions under which this chronicle was printed are very unfavourable to our impression of it, but the opening scenes have not a little of Webster's historical manner.

Webster is conjectured to have written the fine "Induction" to the *Malcontent* of Marston, which was published in 1604, and in 1607 were printed two comedies, in which he had collaborated with Dekker. Of these *Westward Hoe!* was written, perhaps, in 1603, and *Northward Hoe!* in 1605. The hand of Webster is unmistakably prominent in both, Dekker probably supplying but a few farcical scenes. These two plays are brisk and well-constructed, and may rank among the best average comedies of the period. They should be read in conjunction with the *Eastward Hoe!* of Jonson, Chapman, and Marston, printed in 1605; each is in prose. We may continue the list of Webster's works. *The White Devil, or the Life and Death of Vittoria Corombona*, though not published until 1612, was acted about 1608; *Appius and Virginia*, printed first in 1654,

must have been written in 1609, and *The Devil's Law
Case* in 1610, though it did not appear until 1623. *The
Duchess of Malfy*, printed in 1623, was attributed by
Malone, and probably with truth, to 1612. There is no
direct evidence that Webster was connected, after the
last-mentioned year, with the regular stage, although we
find him engaged on a city pageant in 1624, when a
member of his own company was mayor. He was probably the cloth-worker who died in the autumn of 1625.

Webster's masterpiece is *The Duchess of Malfy*, of
which it may confidently be alleged that it is the finest
tragedy in the English language outside the works of
Shakespeare. The poet found his story in that store-
house of plots, the *Novelle* of Bandello, but it had been
told in English by others before him. It was one pre-
eminently suited to inflame the sombre and enthusiastic
imagination of Webster, and to inspire this great,
irregular and sublime poem. Dramatic, in the accepted
sense, it may scarcely be called. In the nice conduct of
a reasonable and interesting plot to a satisfactory con-
clusion, Webster is not the equal of Fletcher or of
Massinger ; some still smaller writers may be considered
to surpass him on this particular ground. But he aimed
at something more, or at least, something other, than
the mere entertainment of the groundlings. With unusual solemnity he dedicates his tragedy to his patron as a
" poem," and his contemporaries perceived that this was
a stronger and more elaborate piece of dramatic architecture than the eye was accustomed to see built for half
a dozen nights, and then disappear. Ford, when he read
The Duchess of Malfy, exclaimed—

> Crown him a poet, whom nor Rome nor Greece
> Transcend in all theirs for a masterpiece,

and Middleton described it as Webster's own monument, fashioned by himself in marble. He had the reputation of being a slow and punctilious writer, among a set of poets, with whom a ready pen was more commonly in fashion. We look to Webster for work designed at leisure, and executed with critical and scrupulous attention. This carefulness, however, was unfavourable to a well-balanced composition, the movement of the whole being sacrificed to an extraordinary brilliancy in detailed passages, and though *The Duchess of Malfy* has again and again been attempted on the modern stage, each experiment has but emphasized the fact that it is pre-eminently a tragic poem to be enjoyed in the study.

It is curious that in a writer so distinguished by care in the working out of detail, we should find so lax a metrical system as marks *The Duchess of Malfy*. Here, again, Webster seems to be content to leave the general surface dull, while burnishing his own favourite passages to a high lustre. He has lavished the beauties both of his imagination and of his verse on what Mr. Swinburne eloquently calls "the overwhelming terrors and the overpowering beauties of that unique and marvellous fourth act, in which the genius of the poet spreads its fullest and darkest wing for the longest and the strongest of its flights."

This is what Bosola ejaculates when the Duchess dies—

> O, she's gone again ! There the cords of life broke.
> O sacred innocence, that sweetly sleeps
> On turtle's feathers, whilst a guilty conscience
> Is a black register wherein is writ

All our good deeds and bad, a perspective
That shows us hell ! that we can not be suffer'd
To do good when we have a mind to it !
This is manly sorrow ;
These tears, I am very certain, never grew
In my mother's milk : my estate is sunk
Below the degree of fear : where were
These penitent fountains while she was living?
O, they were frozen up ! Here is a sight
As direful to my soul as is the sword
Unto a wretch hath slain his father. Come,
I'll bear thee hence,
And execute thy last will ; that's deliver
Thy body to the reverent dispose
Of some good women ; that the cruel tyrant
Shall not deny me. Then I'll post to Milan,
Where somewhat I will speedily enact
Worth my dejection.

The characterization of the Duchess, with her inde-
pendence, her integrity, and her noble and yet sprightly
dignity, gradually gaining refinement as the joy of life is
crushed out of her, is one calculated to inspire pity to
a degree very rare indeed in any tragical poetry. The
figure of Antonio, the subject whom she secretly raises
to a morganatic alliance with her, is simply and whole-
somely drawn. All is original, all touching and moving,
while the spirit of beauty, that rare and intangible
element, throws its charm like a tinge of rose-colour over
all that might otherwise seem to a modern reader harsh
or crude.

On one point, however, with great diffidence, the
present writer must confess that he cannot agree with
those great authorities, Lamb and Mr. Swinburne, who
have asserted, in their admiration for Webster, that he

was always skilful in the introduction of horror.   In his
own mind, as a poet, Webster doubtless was aware of the
procession of a majestic and solemn spectacle, but when
he endeavours to present that conception on the boards
of the theatre, his "terrors want dignity, his affright-
ments want decorum." The horrible dumb shows of
The Duchess of Malfy—the strangled children, the
chorus of maniacs, the murder of Cariola, as she bites
and scratches, the scuffling and stabbing in the fifth act,
are, it appears to me—with all deference to the eminent
critics, who have applauded them—blots on what is notwithstanding a truly noble poem, and what, with more
reserve in this respect, would have been one of the first
tragedies of the world.

Similar characteristics present themselves to us in *The
White Devil*, but in a much rougher form. The
sketchiness of this play, which is not divided into acts
and scenes, and progresses with unaccountable gaps in
the story, and perfunctory makeshifts of dumb show,
has been the wonder of critics. But Webster was
particularly interested in his own work as a romantic
rather than a theatrical poet, and it must be remembered
that after a long apprenticeship in collaboration, *The
White Devil* was his first independent play. It reads as
though the writer had put in only what interested him,
and had left the rest for a coadjutor, who did not happen
to present himself, to fill up. The central figure of
Vittoria, the subtle, masterful, and exquisite she-devil, is
filled up very minutely and vividly in the otherwise
hastily painted canvas; and in the trial-scene, which is
perhaps the most perfectly sustained which Webster has

left us, we are so much captivated by the beauty and
ingenuity of the murderess that, as Lamb says in a
famous passage, we are ready to expect that "all the
court will rise and make proffer to defend her in spite of
the utmost conviction of her guilt." The fascination of
Vittoria, like an exquisite poisonous perfume, pervades
the play, and Brachiano strikes a note, which is the
central one of the romance, when he says to her—

> Thou hast led me like a heathen sacrifice,
> With music and with fatal yokes of flowers,
> To my eternal ruin.

The White Devil is not less full than the *Duchess of
Malfy* of short lines and phrases full of a surprising
melody. In the fabrication of these jewels, Webster is
surpassed only by Shakespeare.

If, as is now supposed, the composition of *Appius and
Virginia* followed closely upon that of *The White Devil*,
it is plain that the reception of the latter play must have
drawn Webster's attention to the necessity of paying
more attention to theatrical requirements. While the
romantic and literary glow of language is severely
restrained, there is here a very noticeable advance in
every species of dramatic propriety, and *Appius and
Virginia* is by far the best constructed of Webster's plays.
The Jacobean dramatists were constantly attempting to
compose Roman tragedies, in which they vaguely saw
the possibility of reaching the classic perfection of form
at which they aimed in their less agitated moments.
Ben Jonson's plays of this class have been already mentioned, and these, to his own contemporaries, seemed to
be by far the most coherent and satisfactory. Posterity,

however, has placed *Julius Cæsar* high above *Sejanus* and
Catiline, and without seeking to put Webster by the
side of Shakespeare, his Roman tragedy must be admitted
to be more graceful, pathetic, and vigorous than Jonson's.

A speech of Virginius in the fourth act will give an
idea of the high Roman tone of the play—

> Have I, in all this populous assembly
> Of soldiers that have proved Virginius' valour,
> One friend ?   Let him come thrill his partizan
> Against this breast, that thro' a large wide wound
> My mighty soul might rush out of this prison,
> To fly more freely to yon crystal palace,
> Where honour sits enthronized.   What, no friend ?
> Can this great multitude, then, yield an enemy
> That hates my life ?   Here let him seize it freely.
> What, no man strike ? am I so well belov'd ?—
> Minertius, then to thee ; if in this camp
> There lives one man so just to punish sin,
> So charitable to redeem from torments
> A ready soldier, at his worthy hand
> I beg a death.

The scenes are largely set, the characters, especially
those of Virginius and of Appius, justly designed and
well contrasted, while the stiffness of Roman manners,
as seen through a Jacobean medium, is not in this case
sufficient to destroy the suppleness of the movement nor
the pathos of the situation. *Appius and Virginia*, as a
poem, will never possess the attractiveness of the two
great Italian romances, but it is the best-executed of
Webster's dramas.

If the playwright took a step forwards in his Roman
play, he took several backwards in his incoherent tragi-
comedy of *The Devil's Law-Case*.   Here no charm

attaches to the characters ; the plot moves around no
central interest ; the structure of the piece, from a stage
point of view, is utterly at fault. None the less, this
strange play will always have its readers, for Webster's
literary faculty is nowhere exhibited to greater perfection,
and the poetry of the text abounds in verbal felicities.
Unfortunately, the special attention of the poet seems
to have been concentrated on the unravelling of a most
fantastic skein of legal intrigues. In listening to the
quibbles and the serpentining subtleties of Ariosto and
Crispiano the reader loses not merely his interest, but
his intelligence ; he is not amused, but merely bewildered.
Leonora, who, to avenge the wrongs of her lover, charges
her own son with illegitimacy, is a being outside the pale
of sympathy.

The abrupt withdrawal of Webster from writing for
the stage—a step which he seems to have taken when
he was little over thirty years of age—points to a sense
of want of harmony between his genius and the theatre.
In fact, none of the leading dramatists of our great
period seems to have so little native instinct for
stage-craft as Webster, and it is natural to suppose that
in another age, and in other conditions, he would have
directed his noble gifts of romantic poetry to other
provinces of the art. If it were not absolutely certain
that he flourished between 1602 and 1612, we should
be inclined to place the period of his activity at least
ten years earlier. Although in fact an exact contemporary
of Beaumont and Fletcher, and evidently much Shakespeare's junior, a place between Marlowe and those
dramatists seems appropriate to him, so primitive is his

theatrical art, so ingenuous and inexperienced his notion of the stage. That he preferred the more stilted and buskined utterances of drama to grace and suppleness may be gathered from Webster's own critical distinctions ; he has no words of admiration too high for Chapman and Jonson ; Shakespeare he commends, with a touch of patronage, on a level with Dekker and Heywood, for his " right happy and copious industry," placing the romantic Beaumont and Fletcher above him. This points to a somewhat academic temper of mind, and to a tendency to look rather at the splendid raiment of drama than at the proficiency and variety of those who wear it. Webster is an impressive rather than a dexterous playwright ; but as a romantic poet of passion he takes a position in the very first rank of his contemporaries.

Of John Day's dramatic works but a small fragment has survived, and it is probable that he appears to us in a very different light from that in which his contemporaries regarded him. He is now quoted as the type and expositor of a playful and delicate side of Jacobean drama, hardly existing elsewhere, a survival or revival of the school of florid conceit and affected pastoral wit, Arcadian and at the same time mundane. But this view of him is largely founded upon the best known of all his productions, the masque entitled *The Parliament of Bees*, and, although so convenient for practical critical purposes as to be not worth disturbing, is probably a quite accidental and non-essential one. Scarcely anything is known of Day's life, except that he was a student of Gonville and Caius College, Cambridge, and that as early as 1598 he was writing plays for

Henslowe. Unless his *Spanish Moor's Tragedy* of 1600 survives as *Lust's Dominion*, of Day's first twenty recorded plays all are lost, except *The Blind Beggar of Bethnal Green*, not published till 1659, but written with Chettle in 1600. This is not an interesting performance, and suggests that we need not deeply regret the destruction of the prentice works of Day.

In 1605 was acted, and in the next year published, *The Isle of Gulls*, a sort of Arcadian satire mainly in prose, " a little spring or rivulet drawn from the full stream " of Sir Philip Sidney's romance. It is curiously Euphuistic, recalling the taste of the end of Elizabeth's reign, very lively in the mechanism of its plot, and the various tricks contrived upon its personages. Mr. Fleay has ingeniously argued that *The Isle of Gulls* was an attack on James I., the duke and duchess being meant for the king and queen. *Law Tricks*, a comedy printed in 1608, was probably some two years earlier acted. Its fault is a certain insipidity ; its merit sweetness of versification and delicacy of fancy. *The Travels of the Three English Brothers*, in which Rowley and Wilkins collaborated with Day, belongs to 1607. *Humour out of Breath*, 1608, is mainly, if not entirely, Day's work. This is, as Mr. Bullen has noted, his most characteristic play. It is a short comedy, in prose, and verse, that is often rhymed ; the spirit and tone of it are plainly copied from those of Shakespeare's romantic comedies. With this play Day's connection with the theatre seems to have ceased. In 1619 Jonson talked about him to Drummond, and said in his haste that Day was " a rogue " and " a base fellow." It is probable that his death occurred in 1640, and we are left to speculate in vain regarding the incidents of a life of perhaps seventy years, with its one decade of feverish professional activity.

In 1641, however, there was posthumously issued the work on which the immortality of Day is supported, his satirical masque of *The Parliament of Bees*. Mr. Fleay has proved that it was touched up for the press by Day himself just before he died ; but to think of this as a work of the extreme old age of Day is impossible. A vague tradition points to 1607 as the year of its composition, and no date could seem more probable for a poem instinct with juvenile elasticity and buoyancy. It is a drama in rhymed ten-syllable and eight-syllable verse, all the characters in which are bees, and converse, as Lamb says, "in words which bees would talk with, could they talk ; the very air seems replete with humming and buzzing melodies, while we read them."

This passage will give an idea of the movement of the dialogue—

> *Prorex.* And whither must these flies be sent?
> *Oberon.* To everlasting banishment.
> Underneath two hanging rocks,
> Where babbling Echo sits and mocks
> Poor travellers, there lies a grove
> With whom the sun's so out of love
> He never smiles on't,—pale Despair
> Calls it his monarchal chair.
> Fruit, half-ripe, hangs rivell'd and shrunk
> On broken arms torn from the trunk :
> The moorish pools stand empty, left
> By water, stolen by cunning theft,
> To hollow banks, driven out by snakes,
> Adders and newts, that man these lakes:

The mossy weeds half swelter'd, serv'd
As beds for vermin, hunger-starv'd :
The woods are yew-trees, rent and broke
By whirlwinds ; here and there an oak
Half cleft with thunder ;—to this grove
We banish them. *All.* Some mercy, Jove !
Oberon. You should have cried so in your youth,
When Chronos and his daughter Truth
Sojourn'd amongst you, when you spent
Whole years in riotous merriment,
Thrusting poor bees out of their hives,
Seizing both honey, wax and lives.

This apian pastoral is one of the most curious and original productions of the age.

Robert Daborne was a playwright of little intrinsic merit, if we may judge by his surviving plays. But he possesses a curious interest for us, as the author of a correspondence with Henslowe which gives "a unique narration of the life of a third-rate dramatist in the pay of an extortionate stage-manager of the time of James I." These letters are nearly thirty in number, and are dated from April 17, 1613, to August 1, 1614. In the course of them we read of Cyril Tourneur, Field, and Massinger as companions in Daborne's misfortunes, and chained to the same theatrical oar. Daborne left the stage in 1614, took holy orders, and proceeded to Waterford, whence he issued a sermon in 1618. His tragedy called *A Christian turned Turk*, 1612, is a wild and inchoate piece of melodrama, founded on a recent case of Levantine piracy ; it contains some vigorous passages. He is thought to have helped Fletcher with *The Honest Man's Fortune.*

Charles Lamb drew attention to a long and very spirited scene in a romantic comedy, called *The Hog hath Lost*

his Pearl, published in 1614. This was written by
Robert Tailor, of whom absolutely nothing else has been
preserved. Tailor's versification is so easy and even,
and the success of his play is so clearly recorded, as to
create surprise at his having, so far as we know, written
for the stage on no other occasion. The central incident
of this remarkably fine piece of work was the crime and
the remorse of a certain Albert, who robs his friend
Carracus of his bride Maria, the pearl which Carracus
has stolen from her father, the old Lord Wealthy.
Nothing whatever is known about Tailor, who wrote his
play to be acted "by certain London prentices." It is
particularly rich in curious theatrical allusions.

John Tomkis, or Tomkins, was a University playwright,
a scholar of Trinity College, Cambridge. Two plays of
his, neither of which is a work of genius, have attracted
a great deal of discussion, and were famous when some
of the masterpieces of Jacobean drama were still unknown.
One of these is *Lingua*, long attributed to Anthony Brewer.
The scene is laid in Microcosmus, in a grove, and the plot
didactically sets forth the combat of the tongue and the
five senses for superiority. Interest was lent to *Lingua*
by the tradition that Oliver Cromwell played in it in the
part of Tactus, and had his political ambition first en-
flamed by it. This play was probably written soon after
the accession of James I., though not published till 1607.
It was very frequently reprinted in the course of the century. Tomkis' other drama, oddly enough, has also been
the centre of a tissue of tradition. *Albumazar*, which was
acted by the gentlemen of Trinity before the king in
1615, and published the same year, attracted the notice

of Dryden, who caused it to be revived, and wrote a prologue for it in 1668. In his enthusiasm for his discovery, Dryden charged Ben Jonson with having chosen *Albumazar* as the model of his own great comedy of *The Alchymist.* This mistake was constantly repeated, in spite of the fact that Jonson's play preceded that of Tomkis by five years.

Certain academic plays of the close of the reign, poems in dramatic form, which were never intended for the public boards, may here be mentioned. Among them the beautiful anonymous tragedy of *Nero*, published as "newly written" in 1624, takes easily the foremost place. No one has been able to form a reasonable conjecture as to the name of the writer, and it is probable that he was young, and never attempted to repeat his experiment. *Nero* is, indeed, what a contemporary critic called it, an "indifferent" acting-play, but is written in unusually good verse, and contains scattered passages which deserve no less enthusiastic epithet than "exquisite."

Thus, in the third act, does Nero give expression to the fatuous vanity of the flattered amateur—

> They tell of Orpheus, when he took his lute
> And moved the noble ivory with his touch,
> Hebrus stood still, Pangæus bowed his head,
> Ossa then first shook off his snow, and came
> To listen to the movings of his song;
> The gentle poplar took the bay along,
> And call'd the pine down from the mountain-seat;
> The virgin-bay, altho' the arts she hates
> Of the Delphic god, was with his voice o'ercome;
> He his twice-lost Eurydice bewails
> And Proserpine's vain gifts, and makes the shores

And hollow caves of forests now untree'd,
Bear his griefs company, and all things teacheth
His lost love's name ; then water, air, and ground
" Eurydice, Eurydice ! " resound.
These are bold tales of which the Greeks have store ;
But if he could from Hell once more return,
And would compare his hand and voice with mine,
Aye, tho' himself were judge, he then would see
How much the Latin stains the Thracian lyre.
I oft have walked by Tiber's flow'ry banks
And heard the swan sing her own epitaph ;
When she heard me, she held her peace and died.

Thomas Goffe, who was born about 1592, and
educated at Christchurch, Oxford, was a clergyman
during the last four years of his life, and died in July,
1627, hen-pecked to death by a wife " who was as great
a plague to him as it was well possible for a shrew to be."
This gentle cleric wrote, before he left Oxford in 1623,
four plays—three tragedies and a tragi-comedy of *The
Careless Shepherdess*—all of which were posthumously
published.   The tragedies, which enjoyed a certain
popularity, were absurdly bombastic and sanguinary,
and recalled the earliest works of such primitives as
Marlowe and Kyd.   The learned Dr. Barton Holiday,
just before he went away to Spain with Gondomar in
1618, produced a play called *Technogamia ; or, The
Marriage of the Arts*, which was acted by the students
in Christchurch Hall on the 13th of February, and four
years later at Woodstock before the king, who was
exceedingly fatigued by it.   Thomas May, who was
born in 1595, and who became a very distinguished prose-
writer and translator in the next reign and during the
Commonwealth, wrote a popular academic comedy, *The*

Heir, and three tragedies, before the close of James I.'s life. He was an active member of the Parliamentarian party, and died in bed, from having fastened his night-cap too tightly under his chin, in 1650. He was one of those whose bodies, after having been buried in West-minster Abbey, were taken up at the Restoration and flung into a pit in the churchyard of St. Margaret's; his monument being, at the same time, taken down from the wall of Poets' Corner.

CHAPTER IX.

A VERY prominent figure among the Jacobean poets, yet one with which it is very difficult to deal, is that of George Wither. The time has passed when this voluminous writer can be treated by any competent critic with the contempt of the age of Anne. The scorn of Pope still clings, however, to the "wretched Withers," whose name he misspelt, and of whose works he had probably seen nothing but the satires. Nor would it be safe, on the score of exquisite beauties discoverable in the early lyrics of Wither, to overlook the radical faults of his style. One or two generous appreciators of Jacobean verse have done this, and have claimed for Wither a very high place in English poetry. But proportion, judgment, taste must count for something, and in these qualities this lyrist was deplorably deficient. The careful student, not of excerpts made by loving and partial hands, but of the bulk of his published writings, will be inclined to hesitate before he admits that Wither was a great poet. He will rather call him a very curious and perhaps unique instance of a tiresome and verbose scribbler, to whom in his youth there came unconsidered flashes of most genuine and exquisite poetry.

George Wither was born at Brantworth, in Hampshire, on the 11th of June, 1588. His parents were in independent and even affluent circumstances; his earliest education was found in the neighbouring village school of Colemore, and he was still but a boy when he was sent to Magdalen College, Oxford. His college career was abruptly terminated after two years, when he returned to "the beechy shadows of Brantworth," and, according to his own possibly hyperbolic statement, " to the plough." The general supposition has been, caused perhaps by some laxity in Anthony à Wood's information, that he went up to London of his own accord in 1605, to seek his fortune there, and entered himself of Lincoln's Inn. The date is probably much too early, for he was then only seventeen years of age, and we know that he spent a weary time in Hampshire. At all events, it is not until 1612 that we hear of him as a poet, and this was probably about the date of his appearance in London. In that year he published, on the theme which excited universal emotion at the moment, a little volume of *Prince Henry's Obsequies*, a series of nearly fifty sonnets, smoothly and volubly indited, and containing occasional phrases of some beauty.

It is understood that this little volume, and a still smaller quarto of *Epithalamia* which immediately followed it, introduced Wither to the company of young poets who at this time began to collect in the courts of law. In particular, it is certain that he gained the friendship of Browne and of Christopher Brooke. In 1613, however,

Wither suddenly became prominent by the publication of a volume of satires entitled *Abuses Stript and Whipt*, of which four editions were rapidly exhausted. The scandal caused by this book was so great that the poet was thrown into the Marshalsea prison, where, as he tells us, he "was shut up from the society of mankind, and, as one unworthy the compassion vouchsafed to thieves and murderers, was neither permitted the use of my pen, the access or sight of acquaintance, the allowances usually afforded other close prisoners, nor means to send for necessaries. . . . I was for many days compelled to feed on nothing but the coarsest bread, and sometimes locked up four and twenty hours together without so much as a drop of water to cool my tongue." This severity must have been presently relaxed, for Wither wrote much in prison ; but he was not suffered to leave the Marshalsea until many months had passed.

It is very difficult, with the text of *Abuses Stript and Whipt* before us, to understand why it should have caused such vehement official resentment. The book is really a collection of essays on ethical subjects, running to about ten thousand verses, all in the heroic couplet. The so-called "satires" deal with such themes as "Love," "Presumption," "Weakness," and "Vanity." There are more odd instances of suppression, of course, than this, that of Drayton's *Harmony of the Church*, being the most unaccountable of all. Wither's satire, however, is so anodyne and so impersonal, so devoid of anything which could, apparently, be taken as a home-thrust by any individual, that the scandal caused by *Abuses Stript and Whipt* is an enigma of literary history. Here are none of those direct portraits which passed almost un-challenged in the satires of Marston and Donne. There is, notwithstanding, a passage in the ninth satire of the first book which attacks the prelates of the English Church very sharply, and the imprudence of this out-burst seems to have struck the poet himself, for he proceeds to a direct flattery of the Archbishop of Canterbury. In the absence of any other light, we may perhaps conjecture that the chapter on "Ambition" earned our young poet his cell in the Marshalsea.

These Satires are readable, and have none of the Persius-like obscurity and roughness of earlier English satire. The author, after some obliging traits of auto-biography, essays to deal with the whole subject of the decay of Man's moral nature. We find lucid con-structions and smooth verse throughout, and wherever a picture of manners is introduced, it is given with a Dutch precision and picturesqueness. Already, in this lively production of his twenty-fifth year, we are conscious of Wither's radical faults, his moral garrulity, his tedious length. It seems certain that the fine lyrical vein in his genius very soon dried up. In the opening of the *Abuses Stript and Whipt*, he speaks of having already indited "Aretophil's compliment, with many doleful sonnets." This collection, then, may be consigned to his very early youth, although, so far as we know, it did not make its public appearance until it was printed, as *Fair Virtue, The Mistress of Philarete*, in 1622. It may be safely dated ten years earlier.

Leaving this collection for awhile, we come to the books which Wither wrote in prison. It is not needful to dwell on his contributions, in 1614, to *The Shepherd's Pipe* of Browne, Christopher Brooke and Davies of Hereford; but in 1615 appeared two exquisite volumes, *Fidelia* and *The Shepherd's Hunting.* The former was privately printed, and of this edition but one copy is known to survive; the latter is not a common book. *Fidelia* is an "elegiacal epistle," in heroic couplet, addressed by a woman to her inconstant friend; it is a fragment of some huge poem probably carried no further. It possesses a great delicacy of passion, and a versification curiously and irresistibly suggestive of that of Dryden; *Fidelia* is by far the most attractive of the non-lyrical works of Wither.

In *The Shepherd's Hunting* all is lyrical in spirit, if not in form. It is divided into eclogues, in which the poet somewhat dimly recounts his woes and their alleviations, in exquisite verse of varied measures. He is not even gloomy long, and hastens to assure us that—

> though that all the world's delight forsake me,
> I have a Muse, and she shall music make me;
> Whose very notes, in spite of closest cages,
> Shall give content to me and after ages.

The fourth eclogue is the sweetest of all. Here, as has been said, "the caged bird begins to sing like a lark at Heaven's gate," and bids its free companions to be of good cheer.

> As the sun doth oft exhale
> Vapours from each rotten vale,
> Poesy so sometimes drains
> Gross conceits from muddy brains,—
> Mists of envy, fogs of spite,
> 'Twixt man's judgments and her light;

> But so much her power may do,
> That she can dissolve them too.
> If thy verse do bravely tower,
> As she makes wing, she gets power ;
> Yet the higher she doth soar,
> She's affronted still the more ;
> Till she to the highest hath past,
> Then she rests with Fame at last.
> Let nought therefore thee affright,
> But make forward in thy flight ;
> For if I could match thy rhyme,
> To the very stars I'd climb,
> There begin anew, and fly
> Till I reached eternity.

In all the days of James I., no more unaffected melodies, no brighter or more aerial notes, were poured forth by any poet than are contained in this delicious little volume of *The Shepherd's Hunting*.

We may now come to the *Mistress of Philarete*. This, as it was finally published, is a much more bulky affair. The form is decidedly unfortunate ; the poem consists of lyrics, many of them of a somewhat miscellaneous character, set in a framework of recitative heroic couplets. The opening of *The Mistress of Philarete*, with its glowing description of the poet's Hampshire home, and in particular of Alresford Pool, has been greatly praised, but can scarcely be praised too highly. Where the contents of this volume are successful, it is in their use of the dancing measure, the true singing note. Nowhere is the octosyllabic used with more rapturous felicity than occasionally here. Often the poet rings out a pure sonorous cadence ; still more often he is rapid, lucid, easy, and modern. If in *Fidelia* we were reminded of Dryden, the double rhymes and reckless

phrases in *Philarete* makes us think of Elizabeth
Browning.

> Say, you purchase, with your pelf,
>   Some respect, where you importune !
> Those may love me, for myself,
>   That regard you for your fortune.
>   Rich, or born of high degree,
>   Fools, as well as you, may be !
>   But that peace in which I live,
>   No descent nor wealth can give.
>
> If you boast that you may gain
>   The respect of high-born beauties,
> Know, I never wooed in vain,
>   Nor preferrèd scornèd duties ;
>   She I love hath all delight,
>   Rosy red with lily white ;
>   And, whoe'er your mistress be,
>   Flesh and blood as good as she.

Wither's diction is curiously transitional here, and
while with one hand he stretches up to Greene and
Lodge, with the other he feels downwards towards the
lyrists of the Restoration.

But it would be utterly uncritical to say this and this
only.   The purple passages are interwoven with the
commonest sacking.   Even in his own day, and thus
early, it had been perceived that he possessed no powers
of self-criticism.   He is very indignant with those who
censure the diffuseness, the length, the didactic dulness
of his poems ; he calls them " fools," and cries—

> Let them know . . .
> I make to please myself, and not for them !

It is a misfortune that he judged himself so ill, for the
" fools " were perfectly right, and all these faults were

patent in his poetry already. They were soon to become paramount, and the darnel was to kill the poetic wheat long before the harvest. The later career of Wither is deplorable. His political and religious tergiversations give the impression, not of hypocrisy in conscious error, but of hopeless blundering, of the wrong-headedness of a radically tactless man. He wrote hymns, which have been over-praised, and he published a multitude of pamphlets in prose and verse, which no one has dared to flatter, and few have tried to read. He outlived James I. by nearly forty years, reaped the reward of his malignant invectives by being lodged in Newgate and in the Tower, and died at last, dishonoured and obscure, on July 27, 1663, as melancholy an instance as we find in literary history of genius outlived, and a beautiful youth belied by a wretched and protracted old age.

At the close of the reign of James I., a verse-writer appeared who almost immediately achieved a popular success phenomenal in its extent. Francis Quarles is a curious figure, and one difficult to define without unfairness. He had but few great qualities of an imaginative kind, and he had many of the faults of the worst authors. He was without distinction and without charm ; he "faggotted his fancies as they fell, and if they rhymed and rattled, all was well." The work was hurriedly, unconscientiously and inartistically done, and he appealed directly to a commonplace audience. Yet he was far from being a writer without merit. His wit—in the seventeenth-century sense—was genuine and sometimes brilliant, and though he has not left behind him one poem which can be read all through with pleasure, he had a large share of the poetic temper, and intervals of rare felicity. He marks the decline in style, and displays broadly enough faults which were characteristic of his generation, and which, it must in fairness be said, he did not a little to foster and extend.

Although the general impression of Quarles is that he was a Puritan, a Nonconformist, and a Radical, the exact opposites were the case. He was a gentleman of good family, a strong Church-and-State man throughout life, a loyal and even impassioned supporter of the king. Such were his private convictions; but the tendency of his multitudinous verses is wholly in the other direction, and if he had been born a little later, it is not easy to believe that he could have failed to be a roundhead. Francis, the third son of James and Joan Quarles, was born at the manor-house of Stewards, in Essex, in May, 1592. His father died when he was seven, and his mother when he was fourteen years of age. From 1605 to 1608 he was at Christ's College, Cambridge, and thence proceeded to Lincoln's Inn. We know not exactly at what period of his youth it was that he served the Queen of Bohemia (as she afterwards became), in the office of cup-bearer, and accompanied her to Germany, but it must have been after her marriage in 1613. He returned to England, and married Ursula Woodgate, in 1618. Soon after this his literary activity began.

In 1620 he seems to have began the rapid series of his verse-publications with *A Feast for Worms*, which is a paraphrase of the book of *Jonah* into heroic couplets, each passage of narrative being succeeded by a "meditatio" of about equal length. The success of this work

led Quarles during the same year to follow it by *Hadassa*,
a paraphrase of the book of *Esther*, cast in precisely the
same form.   In 1624 he published *Job Militant*, which
treated the book of *Job* in identical fashion; and a
volume of *Sion's Elegies*, in which he paraphrased the
prophecy of *Jeremiah* in a slightly different manner, the
book being divided into four "threnodies," each consisting of subdivided sections, of twelve lines each, called
"elegies," but all composed, as before, in heroics.   He
proceeded to treat the *Canticles* in the same way, in his
Sion's Sonnets of 1625, the sections here being of eight
lines, and called "sonnets."   Finally, in a work of his
late life, posthumously published as *Solomon's Recanta-
tion*, he performed the same labour of adaptation on the
book of *Ecclesiastes*, and might, indeed, had his years
been prolonged, have translated the noble prose of the
entire Bible into his jigging and jingling couplets, of
which a citation from *A Feast for Worms* will give a
rather favourable idea—

> To Nineveh he flieth like a roe,
> Each step the other strives to over-go;
> And as an arrow to the mark does fly,
> So bent to flight flies he to Nineveh.
> Now Nineveh a mighty city was,
> Which all the cities of the world did pass;
> A city which o'er all the rest aspires,
> Like midnight Phœbe o'er the lesser fires;
> A city, which, altho' to men was given,
> Better beseemed the majesty of heaven;
> A city great to God, whose angle wall
> Who undertakes to mete with paces shall
> Bring Phœbus thrice abed ere it be done,
> Altho' with dawning Lucifer begun.

> When Jonah had approached the city gate,
> He made no stay to rest nor yet to bait,
> No supple oil his fainting head anoints,
> Stays not to bathe his weather-beaten joints,
> Nor smooth'd his countenance, nor slick't his skin,
> Nor cravèd he the hostage of an inn.

These scriptural paraphrases form the principal contributions of Quarles to purely Jacobean literature. It is said, to be sure, that his secular narrative poem, *Argalus and Parthenia*, was in print as early as 1622, but no one living has seen any edition earlier than the undated one of 1629. It is believed that for nearly twenty years he resided in Ireland, being for part at least of that period secretary to Archbishop Ussher. Soon after his return to England, in 1639, he was made Chronologer to the City of London, a post which he held until his death. Among the best-known of his later writings are his *Samson*, 1631; his *Divine Fancies*, 1632, four books of miscellaneous religious pieces; his famous *Emblems*, 1634-5; and two prose volumes, the *Enchyridion* of 1641, and *The Loyal Convert* of 1643. Quarles died in London on the 8th of September, 1644, and during the succeeding year his widow published a pleasant, but curiously inaccurate and vague memoir of him. The excessive popularity of his most characteristic writings continued long after his death, and fifty years later his hysterical religious lyrics, slightly adapted to baser uses, continued to make their appearance in erotic collections, side by side with the effusions of Rochester and Dorset. In the eighteenth century they revived again, in their legitimate form, and it can scarcely be said that there has been a generation in which Quarles has not still been popular with some portion of the community. Wood was premature in calling him " the sometime darling of the plebeian judgment," for he has never ceased to hold that position.

Quarles' Biblical paraphrases were strange food to be so greedily devoured by men whose fathers had listened to Spenser and Sidney. The dignity and the lucidity of the original narrative disappear entirely, and there is added, to take their place, a moral volubility, a copy-book system of ethics. Prose run mad in couplets is hardly too strong an expression to describe the greater part of these *Hadassas* and *Samsons*, and the ridicule which successive critics have poured on Quarles is not wholly undeserved. He is a slovenly and tasteless writer. But it is undeserved, if it be not toned down, and even mingled with praise. Quarles passes from his rattling loom an immense amount of wretched poetical shoddy, cheap and ugly, but he runs real gold thread through it here and there, and rises on his worst self to occasional good things. His fervour, though it takes such a wearisome form, is genuine, and if he had made the Bible his model, instead of trying to improve upon and popularize the text itself, he might often have succeeded. As Fuller says, Quarles "had a mind biassed to devotion."

It was where he trusted to his own invention that he showed his best side. His elegies on the deaths of private persons, of which he published seven or eight, are steeped in Biblical phraseology, and here, where he is no longer trying to versify the dignified prose of the

Scriptures, he is occasionally very felicitous. But he is also inspired here, and to his advantage, by the elegiac writings of Donne, with which he must have met in manuscript. This passage, for instance, from *An Alphabet of Elegies upon Dr. Aylmer,* is directly derived from the mode of that potent master—

> Go, glorious saint ! I knew 'twas not a shrine
> Of flesh could lodge so pure a soul as thine ;
> I saw it labour, in a holy scorn
> Of living dust and ashes, to be sworn
> A heavenly chorister ; it sighed and groaned
> To be dissolved from mortal, and enthroned
> Among his fellow-angels, there to sing
> Perpetual anthems to his heavenly king.

But where Quarles is entirely himself is in a kind of vigorous, homely wit, a bending of common language to suit exalted ideas. The *Elegy on Sir Edmund Wheeler,* for instance, contains this reflection, which would have occurred to none but Quarles—

> So vain, so frail, so poor a thing is Man !
> A weathercock that's turn'd with every blast ;
> His griefs are armfuls, and his mirth a span ;
> His joys soon crost or passed ;
> His best delights are sauced with doubts and fears ;
> If bad, we plunge in care, if lost, in tears ;
> Let go or held, they bite ; we hold a wolf by th' ears.

The least imperfect passage of serious poetry to be found in the works of Quarles, occurs, perhaps, in the *Mildreiados,* an elegy on the death of Mildred, Lady Luckyn—

Oh ! but this light is out ! what wakeful eyes
 E'er marked the progress of the queen of light,
Robed with full glory in her austrian skies,
 Until at length in her young noon of night,
 A swart tempestuous cloud doth rise, and rise,
 And hides her lustre from our darken'd sight ;
Even so, too early death, that has no ears
Open to saints, in her scarce noon of years,
Dashed out our light, and left the tempest in our tears.

After quoting this, it is perhaps not unfair to show the
other side of the medal, and exemplify Quarles at a
less happy moment. This is how, in the secular poem of
Argalus and Parthenia, an intemperate lady succumbs to
excess of feeling—

Her blistered tongue grows hot, her liver glows,
Her veins do boil, her colour comes and goes,
She staggers, falls, and on the ground she lies,
Swells like a bladder, roars, and bursts, and dies.

This scarcely sounds so passionate as the poet hoped
it would.

An isolated figure in the literature of the age is Fulke
Greville, Lord Brooke, who was born earlier than any
other writer included in the scope of this volume, but
who composed the poetry of his which we possess,
mainly, in all probability, in the reign of James I.
Lord Brooke's verse is unsympathetic and unattrac-
tive, yet far too original and well-sustained to be overlooked. He is like one of those lakes, which exist here
and there on the world's surface, which are connected
with no other system of waters, and by no river contribute to the sea. Lord Brooke's abstruse and acrid
poetry proceeded from nowhere and influenced no one.

It is a solitary phenomenon in our literature, and the author a kind of marsupial in our poetical zoology. In the breadth of his sympathy for everything written between 1580 and 1630, Charles Lamb embraced Lord Brooke's strange poems and plays. It is not possible to improve on the verdict of this admirable critic ; Lamb says of Lord Brooke :—" He is nine parts Machiavel and Tacitus, for one part Sophocles or Seneca. In this writer's estimation of the faculties of his own mind, the understanding must have held a most tyrannical pre-eminence. Whether we look into his plays, or his most passionate love-poems, we shall find all frozen and made rigid with intellect." It is quite incredible that Lord Brooke's poetry should ever become popular, but it deserves as much attention as can be given to work essentially so unexhilarating.

Fulke Greville was born at Beauchamp Court, in Warwickshire, in 1554. In November, 1564, he proceeded to Shrewsbury School, where was entered, on the some day, a boy named Philip Sidney, whose intimate friend and biographer he was destined to become. They were, however, separated after their school-life was over, for while Sidney went to Oxford, Greville became a fellow-commoner at Jesus College, Cambridge, in 1568. Later on, in the court of Elizabeth, he renewed his companionship with Sir Philip Sidney, and became intimate with Sir Edward Dyer. Sidney celebrates their enthusiastic affection in several well-known poems—

> Welcome my two to me,
> The number best beloved ;
> Within my heart you be
> In friendship unremoved ;

Join hands and hearts, so let it be,
Make but one mind in bodies three.

While Dyer and Sidney, however, applied themselves early to poetry, and took part in the prosodical revolutions of the Areopagus, Greville seems to have refrained from verse, or else, what he wrote has not come down to us. At all events, his existing works app'ear to belong, in the main, to the post-Elizabethan period; the cycle of *Cælica*, which seems to date from the close of the sixteenth century, being excepted. He was a very scanty contributor to the Elizabethan miscellanies. His interests, in fact, seem to have been mainly political, and after the death of Sidney, Greville rose to high honours in the state. As early as 1576 he began to receive offices in Wales, and before he was thirty, he had been made secretary for the whole principality. In 1597 he was knighted. It has been supposed that his fortunes sustained some check at the accession of James I., but this must have been very temporary, for we find him confirmed for life in his Welsh office, and in 1614 raised to the position of Chancellor of the Exchequer. He was made a peer in 1620, but was never married. The young William Davenant was brought up in his service; and Lord Brooke was, indeed, throughout his career, though accused of extreme parsimony, the patron of poets and scholars. In September, 1628, in circumstances which have remained very obscure, Lord Brooke was murdered in his London house in Holborn, by a serving-man of the name of Haywood, who stabbed him in the back in his bed-chamber, and then committed suicide before he could be brought to justice.

Lord Brooke published nothing during his own life-time, for the edition of his tragedy of *Mustapha*, which appeared in 1609, was almost certainly issued against his will. Five years after his death was printed, in a small folio, *Certain Learned and Elegant Works*, 1633, a collection which comprised the treatises *Of Human Learning*, *Upon Fame and Honour*, and *Of Wars*, the tragedies of *Alaham* and *Mustapha*, the lyrical cycle of a hundred and nine poems called *Cælica*, and some prose miscellanies. So late as 1670 appeared *The Remains of Fulk Greville, Lord Brooke*, being the *Treatises of Monarchy and Religion*. These two volumes contain, with very trifling exceptions, the entire poetical works of Lord Brooke, his famous prose life of Sir Philip Sidney being also posthumous. It is a vexed question when these works were written. The publisher of 1633 averred that " when he grew old he revised the poems and treatises he had wrote long before," but this is very vague. The collection called *Cælica* has something of an Elizabethan character ; the rest seem undoubtedly, both by external and internal evidence, to belong to the seventeenth century. The *Treatise of Monarchy*, for instance, could not have been written till some years after the accession of James.

A great monotony of style marks the poetry of Lord Brooke. It is harsh and unsympathetic ; the verse, which depends for life on its stateliness alone, sinks, between the purple passages, to a leaden dulness. The " treatises " are exceedingly difficult to read through. They all begin—and this is a very curious point—with an eloquent stanza or two, only to sink immediately into a jog-trot of prose in lengths. One or two critics have

chosen to praise Lord Brooke with something like
extravagance.   It is true that he is full of ripe and
solemn thought; it is not less true that he is always
endeavouring to present to us noble views of character
and conduct.   As Phillips said, in his *Theatrum
Poetarum* of 1675, Lord Brooke has "a close, mysterious,
and sententious way of writing."   But, except here and
there in the course of *Cælica*, he entirely forgets that the
poet has to be an artist; he thinks of him purely as a
teacher, and as a prophet.   He does not shrink from
such lines as—

> Knowledge's next organ is imagination,

or from rhyming "heart" with "arts," and alternating
"pain" and "gain" by "fame" and "frame."   His
dignity, his earnestness, his religious and moral senten-
tiousness are unilluminated by colour, imagery, or melody.

> Two sects there be in this earth, opposite;
>   The one makes Mahomet a deity,—
> A tyrant Tartar raised by war and sleight,
>   Ambitious ways of infidelity;
>   The world their heaven is, the world is great,
>   And racketh those hearts when it has receipt.
>
> The other sect of cloister'd people is,
>   Less with the world, with which they seem to war,
> And so in less things drawn to do amiss,
>   As all lusts less than lust of conquest are;
>   Now if of God both these have but the name
>   What mortal idol then can equal Fame?

In his bold political speculations and his reflections
on the effects of tyranny taken from ancient history and

modern experience, he sometimes reminds us of Sir John Davies, but at a great distance.

His plays are what Lamb described them to be, frozen. He tells us that he wrote others, to which he intended his elaborate didactic "treatises" to serve as choruses; and in particular he burned with his own hand an *Antony and Cleopatra* which it would have been amusing to compare with Shakespeare's. The two we possess are, however, all that we can desire, and few have had the patience to read them. They are, in some measure, composed upon the Seneca model. *Alaham* opens with a long rhymed prologue of sonorous irregular stanza, spoken by the ghost of a murdered King of Ormuz, descriptive of hell.

This is how it begins :—

> Thou monster horrible, under whose ugly doom,
> Down in Eternity's perpetual night,
> Man's temporal sins bear torments infinite,
> For change of desolation, must I come
> To tempt the earth and to profane the light,
> From mournful silence whose pain dares not roar,
> With liberty to multiply it more?
> Nor from the loathsome puddle Acheron
> Made foul with common sins, whose filthy damps
> Feed Lethe's sink, forgetting all but moan,
> Nor from that foul infernal shadowed lamp
> Which lighteth Sisyphus to roll his stone,—
> These be but bodies' plagues, the skirts of hell ;
> I come from whence Death's seat doth Death excell.
> A place there is upon no centre plac'd,
> Deep under depths as far as is the sky
> Above the earth, dark, infinitely spac'd ;
> Pluto, the King, the kingdom, Misery:
> The crystal may God's glorious seat resemble,
> Horror itself these horrors but dissemble.

Some of these choruses, in a long broken metre, must, even then, have seemed exceedingly old-fashioned. *Mustapha* is an easier play to follow, and Mrs. Humphrey Ward has drawn attention to the almost Miltonic magnificence of the Chorus of Tartars at the end of the fifth act.

> Vast superstition ! glorious style of weakness !
> Sprung from the deep disquiet of man's passion,
> To desolation and dispair of nature !
> The texts bring princes' titles into question ;
> Thy prophets set on work the sword of tyrants ;
> They manacle sweet Truth with their distinctions ;
> Let Virtue blood ; teach cruelty for God's sake ;
> Fashioning one God, yet him of many fashions ;
> Like many-headed Error in their passions.

Mustapha has less rhyme introduced into it than *Alaham*, and has a somewhat more modern air. Human interest and the play of the emotions are entirely neglected in these curious wooden dramas.

Equally abstruse, and, I fear it must be acknowledged, equally difficult to enjoy, are the tragedies of William Alexander, of Menstrie, afterwards Earl of Stirling. He was born about 1580, and early became a friend and fellow-student of James I. He has been called "the econd-rate Scotch sycophant of an inglorious despotism," but this is needlessly severe. Like so many of his contemporaries, he celebrated the real or imaginary loves of his youth in a thin volume of songs and sonnets called *Aurora*, printed in 1604. Before this, in 1603, he had published in Edinburgh his tragedy of *Darius*. To this followed *Cræsus* in 1604, and *The Alexandræan* in 1605. He reprinted these, and added a *Julius Cæsar*, in 1607, calling the collection *Four Monarchic Tragedies.* He issued an *Elegy on Prince Henry* in 1612, and a religious poem called *Doomsday* in 1614. His writings, strange to say, were popular, and were frequently reprinted during his lifetime. In 1621 Alexander was knighted; in 1626 he was appointed Secretary for Scotland; in 1630 he was created Viscount Canada, in recognition of his colonial services; and in 1633 was made Earl of Sterling. He died in 1640. Stiff and pedantic as he is, and without the intellectual weight of Lord Brooke, Alexander by no means deserves the contempt which has been thrown upon him. The *Aurora* contains several sonnets and madrigals which are little inferior to the best of Drummond's, and even the mail-clad versification of the "monarchic tragedies" is often melodious and stately.

CHAPTER X.

PHILIP MASSINGER.

NOTHING exemplifies more curiously the rapidity of development in poetical literature at the opening of the seventeenth century than the fact that the same brief reign which saw the last perfection placed on the edifice of Elizabethan drama saw also the products of the pen of Massinger. For, however much we may respect the activity of this remarkable man, however warmly we may acknowledge the power of his invention, the skill and energy with which he composed, and however agreeable his plays may appear to us if we compare them with what succeeded them in a single generation, there can be no question that the decline in the essential parts of poetry from Webster or Tourneur, to go no further back, to Massinger is very abrupt. Mr. Leslie Stephen has noted in this playwright "a certain hectic flush, symptomatic of approaching decay," and we may even go further and discover in him a leaden pallor, the sign of decreasing vitality. The "hectic flush" seems to me to belong more properly to his immediate successors, who do not come within the scope of this volume, to Ford, with his morbid sensibility, and to Shirley, with his mechanical ornament, than to Massinger, where the decline chiefly shows itself in the negation of qualities, the absence of what is brilliant, eccentric, and passionate. The sentimental and rhetorical drama of Massinger has its excellent points, but it is dominated by the feeling that the burning summer of poetry is over, and that a russet season is letting us down gently towards the dull uniformity of winter. Interesting and specious as Massinger is, we cannot avoid the impression that he is preparing us for that dramatic destitution which was to accompany the Commonwealth.

So much of Massinger's work appeared in the reign of Charles I., that he may perhaps be considered as scarcely Jacobean. But when we bear in mind the long apprenticeship he served with Fletcher and others, and if we regard, not the published dates of his principal plays, but the years in which they must reasonably be supposed to have been acted, we come to think of Massinger as not merely unalienably Jacobean, but as the leading poet of the close of James's reign. He was born at Salisbury, and was baptized at St. James's on the 24th of November, 1583, being thus nineteen years younger than Shakespeare and ten years than Ben Jonson. His father, whose name was Arthur, "happily spent many years, and died a servant" to the family of the Herberts, but he was "*generosus*," and much respected by the heads of the clan which he thus "served" in delicate matters of business. It has been supposed that Sir Philip Sidney was the god-father of the poet, and that the boy became page to the Countess of Pembroke, but these are matters of mere conjecture.

That he was brought up in or near Wilton, and was familiar with the stately occupants of that great house, may, at all events, be taken for certain.

On the 14th of May, 1602, Philip Massinger was entered as a commoner of St. Alban's Hall, Oxford. Wood gives us the impression that the Earl of Pembroke was disappointed in the lad, who "gave his mind more to poetry and romances for about four years and more, than to logic and philosophy, which he ought to have done, as he was patronized to that end." Langbaine, a poorer witness, denies this, saying that he was industrious, and that his father alone supported his charges. But he took no degree when he left Oxford in 1606, abruptly, owing either to his father's death or to the withdrawal of the Herbert patronage. Gifford supposed that Massinger had lost favour by becoming a Roman Catholic; the fact is in itself not certain, but it is made highly probable by the tone of several of his compositions. Wood says that on reaching London, Massinger, "being sufficiently famed for several specimens of wit, betook himself to writing plays." The "specimens of wit" have not come down to us, and we are unable to trace, for many years, the plays he wrote. But there is reason to believe that he lived in extreme poverty, and that his literary labours were for a long time restricted to partnership with luckier playwrights and to the re-modelling of old, discarded dramas of the Elizabethan age.

There exist signs that in 1613 Massinger was employed in writing plays with Fletcher and Field, and a little later with Daborne also. The earliest work in which his hand can certainly be traced is *The Fatal Dowry*, which he wrote in conjunction with Field about 1619. The *Very Woman* was performed at Court in 1621. But we possess the names of seven plays, all of which came into Warburton's hands, and were burned by his egregious cook—three tragedies, three comedies, and one tragi-comedy. All these, it seems probable, were written by Massinger without help from any author, before 1620. In thirteen or fourteen of Fletcher's plays, too, he had a hand or at least a main finger. Of all this large section of his work it is obvious that no criticism can be attempted, for all must be conjecture. Of his re-modelling of plays, *The Virgin Martyr* is the one clearly defined example, and in this instance it cannot be said that Massinger shines as a poet by comparison with Dekker. All this time, he was probably very poor. When he was forty years of age, we find him piteously begging to be relieved by a loan of five pounds.

The earliest play which is known to survive in which Massinger was not assisted by any other poet is *The Duke of Milan*, which was published, with a dedication to Lady Catherine Stanhope, in 1623, but probably acted about three years earlier. This marked the starting-point of a period during which Massinger broke away, we cannot guess for what reason, from the bondage of working under Fletcher, and determined, already rather late in life, to show that he could carry through a play unaided. Perhaps his next experiment was *The Maid of Honour*, although that was not published until 1632. *A New Way to Pay Old Debts* (printed 1632) could not have preceded, and yet must soon have followed the scandal about Sir Giles Mompesson in 1620. To the same period has been ascribed *The Unnatural Combat.* There may then have been a pause in Massinger's activity, or he returned to his work of collaboration with Fletcher; but four important dramas seem to belong to the closing years of the life of James I. These are *The Bondman,* published in 1624, *The Renegado, The Parliament of Love,* and *The Great Duke of Florence.* If those are correct who believe all these plays to have been produced on the boards before 1625, the question of the propriety of considering Massinger as a Jacobean poet is settled. He thought that he continued to improve, and that *The Roman Actor* was " the most perfect birth of my Minerva." But the truth is that we should be admirably acquainted with all his qualities and his defects if his career had closed with that of James I. As a matter of fact, he continued to live on until the 17th of March, 1638, when he was found dead in the morning in his house on the Bankside. His body was buried next day in St. Saviour's, Southwark, in the grave already occupied by the dust of John Fletcher. His later plays included *The Picture, The City Madam, Believe as you List, The Emperor of the East,* and *The Bashful Lover.*

The comparison has been made between Massinger and such earlier poets as Webster. This is a parallel which, from our present standpoint, militates strongly against the first-named writer. For, if the truth be told, Massinger is scarcely a poet, except in the sense in which that word may be used of any man who writes seriously in dramatic form. What we delight in in the earlier Elizabethans, the splendid bursts of imaginative insight, the wild freaks of diction, the sudden sheet-lightning of poetry illuminating for an instant dark places of the soul, all this is absent in Massinger.   He is uniform and humdrum ; he has no lyrical passages ; his very versification, as various critics have observed, is scarcely to be distinguished from prose, and often would not seem metrical if it were printed along the page.   Intensity is not within his reach, and even in the aims of composition we distinguish between the joyous instinctive lyricism of the Elizabethans, which attained to beauty without much design, and this deliberate and unimpassioned work, so plain and easy and workmanlike.   It is very natural, especially for a young reader, to fling Massinger to the other end of the room, and to refuse him all attention.

This is unphilosophical and ungenerous.   If we shift our standpoint a little, there is much in the author of *The Renegado* which demands our respect and insures our enjoyment.   If he be less brilliant than these fiery poets, if his pictures of life do not penetrate us as theirs do, he has merits of construction which were unknown to them.   The long practice which he had in prentice work was none of it thrown away upon him.   It made him, when once he gained confidence to write alone, an admirable artificer of plays.   He is the Scribe of the seventeenth century.   He knows all the tricks by which curiosity is awakened, sustained, and gratified.   He composes, as few indeed of his collaborators seem to have done, not for the study so much as for the stage.   He perceived, we cannot doubt, certain faults in that noble dramatic literature of Fletcher's with which he was so long identified. He perceived Fletcher's careless exaggeration and his light ideal. It was Massinger who recalled English drama to sobriety and gravity.

The absence of bloody violence in his plays must strike every reader, and at the same time the tendency to introduce religious and moral reflections. The intellectual force of Massinger was extolled by Hazlitt, and not unjustly, but it was largely exercised in smoothing out and regulating his conceptions. The consequence is that Massinger tends to the sentimental and the rhe'orical, and that description takes the place of passion. His characters too often say, in their own persons, what it should have been left for others to say of them. Variety of interest is secured, but sometimes at the sacrifice of evolution, and the personages act, not as human creatures must, but as theatrical puppets should. His humour possesses the same fault as his seriousness, that it is not intense. Without agreeing with Hartley Coleridge, who said that Massinger would be the worst of all dull jokers, if Ford had not contrived to be still duller, it must be admitted that the humour of Massinger is seldom successful unless when it is lambent and suffused, when, that is to say, it tinctures a scene rather than illuminates a phrase. In short, Massinger depends upon his broad effects, whether in comedy or tragedy, and must not be looked to for jewels ten words long. His songs have been the scoff of criticism; they really are among the worst ever written. He was, in short, as cannot be too often repeated, essentially unlyrical, yet his plays have great merits. They can always be read with ease, for they seem written with decorum; as Charles Lamb said, they are characterized by "that equability of all the passions, which made his English style the purest and most free from violent metaphors and harsh constructions, of any of the dramatists who were his contemporaries."

Further insight into the qualities of Massinger's work may perhaps be gained by a more detailed examination of one or two of his dramas. By general consent, the best written and the most characteristic of his tragedies is *The Duke of Milan*, the most solid and brilliant of his comedies *A New Way to Pay Old Debts*. In the former of these plays, Sforza, the Duke, is newly married to Marcelia, whom he loves with a frantic and almost maniacal uxoriousness. His delight in the Duchess is felt to be ridiculous and odious in its excess by his mother Isabella and his sister Mariana, who are, however, kept at bay by Francisco, a nobleman married to Mariana, and the Duke's especial favourite. Forced by the approach of the Emperor Charles to go forth to meet and avert his conquering army, Sforza tears himself from Marcelia, but not until he has wrung from Francisco, whom he leaves as regent, an oath that if his death should be reported, Francisco shall instantly kill Marcelia, whom Sforza cannot bear to think of as surviving him. During the Duke's absence, Francisco dishonourably makes love to the Duchess, and, to prejudice her against her husband, divulges this monstrous plan. Sforza comes back safe and sound, but observes at once the natural coldness of Marcelia, who does not appreciate having thus been doomed to execution. The play closes in violent and ferocious confusion; but that was the taste of the time. It is clearly constructed, the plot is lucidity itself, and the first act, as is usual with Massinger, is admirably devised to put the spectator in possession of all the necessary facts.

When, however, we come to reflect upon the conduct of this plausible drama, we find much which calls for unfavourable comment. There has been a great deal of bustle and show, and an interesting spectacle, but no play of genuine character. If, as has been conjectured, it was Massinger's intention deliberately to emulate Shakespeare in *Othello*, his failure is almost ludicrous. The figures are strongly contrasted, and they play at cross-purposes; did they not do so, the tragedy would come to a stand-still; their inconsistencies are the springs of the movement. Hazlitt and others have found great fault with the conception of Sforza, as being irrelevant and violent. It is not needful, however, to go so far as this in censure. It may surely be admitted that Sforza is a credible type of the neuropathic Italian despot. His agitation in the first act is true and vivid; his moods are those of a man on the verge of madness, but they do not cross that verge.

He reaches the highest pitch of hysterical agitation in the fine scene in the fifth act, where the dead body of Marcelia is brought across the stage—

> Carefully, I beseech you :
> The gentlest touch ; and then think
> What I shall suffer.   O you earthly gods,
> You second natures, that from your great master,
> Who join'd the limbs of torn Hippolytus
> And drew upon himself the Thunderer's envy,
> Are taught those hidden secrets that restore
> To life death-wounded men !   You have a patient

On whom to express the excellence of art
Will bind even Heaven your debtor, tho' it pleases
To make your hands the organs of the work
The saints will smile to look on, and good angels
Clap their celestial wings to give it plaudits.
How pale and worn she looks ! O, pardon me,
That I presume (dyed o'er with bloody guilt,
Which makes me, I confess, far, far unworthy),
To touch this snow-white hand.   How cold it is !
This once was Cupid's firebrand, and still
'Tis so to me.   How slow her pulses beat too !
Yet in this temper she is all perfection,
And mistress of a heat so full of sweetness,
The blood of virgins in their pride of youth
Are balls of snow or ice compar'd unto her.

The real fault of *The Duke of Milan* is not the
unnaturalness of Sforza, but the fact that the dramatist
has limited his attention to him. The remoteness of
the Duke's passions, his nervous eccentricities, should
have forced Massinger to keep all the characters at
a low and quiet pitch, so to contrast the neurosis of
Sforza with their normal condition. But all the other
characters are no less frenzied than he is, without his
excuses. The abrupt wooing of Francisco, who is a
mere shadow of Iago, in the second act, is utterly untrue ;
his equally abrupt repentance, in the third act, is not less
extraordinary, and is introduced for no other reason than
that Marcelia should know Sforza's plan for her being
killed in case he does not return alive. If we turn to
the female characters, they are not more natural ; the
mother and sister of the Duke are vulgar scolds, Marcelia
herself utterly ugly and absurd. Everything is extreme
and yet weak ; the characters are made of india-rubber,

and the dramatist presses them down or pulls them out as he sees fit. His study of Sforza is carefully executed, and has passages of great suavity and charm—such as his meeting with the Emperor Charles—but to the evolution of this single character the entire play is sacrificed.

This speech of Sforza, when introduced to the Emperor Charles, is one of the best things in the play—

> If example
> Of my fidelity to the French, whose honours,
> Titles, and glories, are now mixed with yours,
> As brooks, devoured by rivers, lose their names,
> Has power to invite you to make him a friend,
> That hath given evident proof he knows to love,
> And to be thankful: this my crown, now yours,
> You may restore me, and in me instruct
> These brave commanders, should your fortune change,
> Which now I wish not, what they may expect
> From noble enemies for being faithful.
> The charges of the war I will defray,
> And what you may, not without hazard, force,
> Bring freely to you; I'll prevent the cries
> Of murder'd infants and of ravish'd maids,
> Which in a city sack'd, call on Heaven's justice,
> And stop the course of glorious victories:
> And when I know the captains and the soldiers,
> That have in the lost battle done best service,
> And are to be rewarded, I myself,
> According to their quality and merits,
> Will see them largely recompens'd.—I have said,
> And now expect the sentence.

When we turn from this tragedy to the comedy of *A New Way to Pay Old Debts*, we are struck by similar characteristics, modified, however, by the fact that this is

a much stronger and more vivid play than *The Duke of
Milan.* At the outset we are interested to find ourselves
on a scene so frankly English and modern. Massinger
had much of the spirit of the journalist, and it has been
pointed out by Mr. Gardiner and others that he was
constantly engaged in referring to events of passing
politics. Here he was inspired by a sensational case
which had but recently engaged the notice of the courts
of law, and the comedy palpitates with topical allusions.
The plot of the play is clear and interesting. Sir Giles
Overreach, a self-made man, by alternately wheedling and
bullying the lax gentry of the country-side, has ruined
them all, and rules the whole neighbourhood. In
particular, he has so cleverly played on the illusions and
the vices of young Wellborn, the squire, that he has
stripped him of everything, and the generous Wellborn
has to appear among his late tenants in rags. Overreach
has no son, but one daughter, and his design is to marry
her to Lord Lovell, the local grandee, and so finally
secure his own position in the county. He is over-
tricked, however, by a rich and eccentric widow, Lady
Allworth, who patronizes Wellborn, the prodigal, and
marries Lord Lovell herself. The intrigue of the last
act, in which Wellborn constrains Overreach to give him
the money with which he pays his old debts, gives name
to the play, but is somewhat obscurely managed. Notwithstanding this, however, *A New Way to Pay Old
Debts* is the example of the entire Elizabethan and
Jacobean drama outside Shakespeare which has longest
held its place on the modern stage.

As is customary with Massinger, the first act is singularly skilful. The story told in sarcasm to Wellborn by Tapwell, the rascally innkeeper, is exactly what we need to put us in possession of the facts. Wellborn's condition, character, and prospects are placed before us in absolute clearness, our sympathies are engaged, and the little mystery of his whisper to the lady, at the close of the act, is left dark so as to freshen and carry on our curiosity. In the second act, we begin to appreciate the force and cunning of Sir Giles Overreach, in whose wickedness there is something colossal that impresses the imagination. The third act sustains this impression and even increases it, but after this the threads become, not exactly entangled, but twisted, and the illusion of nature is gradually lost. In *A New Way to Pay Old Debts* that unhappy forcible-feebleness of Massinger's is not so strikingly prominent as elsewhere, yet we see something of it in Marall's crude and abrupt temptation of Wellborn to commit some crime and so put an end to his miseries. A certain Justice Greedy pervades the piece, a magistrate who is always raging for his food. Some critics have thought his gluttonies very diverting, but Massinger borrowed them directly from Beaumont and Fletcher, and they are too incessant not to become fatiguing. The charm of this play, after all, consists in its realistic picture of English country life in 1620, and in its curious portrait of the great savage parvenu, eater of widows and orphans, a huge machine for unscrupulous avarice and tyranny. In Sir Giles Overreach, Massinger approaches more nearly than anywhere else to a dramatic creation of the first order.

Little would be gained by examining with the like

minuteness the rest of Massinger's dramas.   For so brief
a sketch as we must here confine ourselves to, it is
enough to say that in the main they present the same
characteristics.   This playwright commonly shows a
capacity for depicting courtly and gentle persons, engaged
in pleasant converse amongst themselves.   For suavity
and refinement of this kind, *The Grand Duke of Florence*
is remarkable.   Lamb has praised *The Picture* for " good
sense, rational fondness, and chastened feeling ; " this
is true of its execution, but hardly of its repulsive central
idea.   On the whole, Massinger may be commended for
the prominence and the dignity which he readily assigns
to women ; but in attempting to show them independent,
he not unfrequently paints them exceedingly coarse and
hard.   His political bias was towards a kind of oligarchic
liberalism ; Coleridge describes him as " a decided
Whig."   Sometimes he indulged this tendency in politics
by satirizing the ladies of a less aristocratic walk of life
than he usually affected, and *The City Madam* is a lively
example of his gifts in this direction.   The diction of
the dramatist is particularly rich in the last-named play,
and Massinger has not written better verse than this
from Luke's soliloquy in the third act—

> Thou dumb magician [*taking out a key*] that without a charm
> Didst make my entrance easy, to possess
> What wise men wish and toil for !   Hermes' Moly,
> Sibylla's golden bough, the great elixir
> Imagin'd only by the alchymist,
> Compar'd with thee are shadows,—thou the substance,
> And guardian of felicity !   No marvel
> My brother made thy place of rest his bosom,
> Thou being the keeper of his heart, a mistress

To be hugg'd ever ! In bye-corners of
This sacred room, silver in bags, heap'd up
Like billets saw'd and ready for the fire,
Unworthy to hold fellowship with bright gold
That flow'd about the room, conceal'd itself.
There needs no artificial light ; the splendour
Makes a perpetual day there, night and darkness
By that still-burning lamp for ever banished !
But when, guided by that, my eyes had made
Discovery of the caskets, and they opened,
Each sparkling diamond from itself shot forth
A pyramid of flames, and in the roof
Fix'd it a glorious star, and made the place
Heaven's abstract or epitome ! Rubies, sapphires,
And ropes of orient pearl, these seen, I could not
But look on with contempt.

When the directly Gallic fashion of the Restoration had
gone out, and dramatists had turned once more to their
Jacobean predecessors, Massinger came back into favour.
His example had much to do in forming the style of such
sentimental tragic writers as Rowe and Lillo, and again,
a century later, his influence was paramount on Talfourd
and Sheridan Knowles.   He has always been easy to
imitate, and it may be said that until Lamb began to
show quite clearly what the old English drama really
was, most readers vaguely took their impression of it
from the pages of Massinger.   He was succeeded, it is
true, by several younger playwrights, particularly by
Ford, Shirley, and Brome ; but each of these—all poets
whose works lie outside the scope of the present volume
—returned closer than he did to the tradition of their
fathers.   Massinger is, really, though not technically and
literally, the last of the great men.   In him we have all
the characteristics of the school in their final decay,

before they dissolved and were dispersed. At the same time, it must never be forgotten that we do not know what he may have been capable of in his youth, and that he was nearly forty, and therefore possibly beyond his poetic prime, before he wrote the earliest play which has come down to us. If Warburton's miserable cook had not burned *Minerva's Sacrifice* and *The Italian Nightpiece,* we might, possibly, put Massinger on a higher level; but criticism can make no conjectures, and we must place the worthy and industrious playwright where we find him.

INDEX.

A

Abuses Stript and Whipt,
Wither, 183, 184
Agincourt, Ballad of, 96
——, *Battle of*, 97
Alaham, Lord Brooke, 199, 200
Albumazar, Tomkis, 177, 178
Alchymist, The, Ben Jonson,
24, 27–30, 33, 178
Alexander, Sir William, of
Menstrie, 106, 200, 201
All's Lost by Lust, Rowley, 130
Amends for Ladies, Field, 87,
88
Anatomy of the World, An,
J. Donne, 48
Ancrum, Robert Ker, Earl of,
106
Anthologies, Elizabethan, 6
Antony and Cleopatra, Shake-
speare, 20
——, Lord Brooke, 199
Appius and Virginia, Webster,
165, 170, 171
Argalus and Parthenia, Quarles,
191, 194
Arnim, Robert, 113

Atheist's Tragedy, The, Tour-
neur, 159, 162–164
Aubrey, John, 83
Aurora, Alexander, 200, 201
Aytoun, Sir Robert, 106

B

Bandello's *Novelle*, 132, 166
Barkstead, William, 22, 112,
113
Barnabae Itinerarium, R. Brath-
wait, 109–112
Barnes, Barnaby, 9, 102
Barnfield, Richard, 5
Baron's Wars, The, Drayton,
94
Barry, Lodowick, 132
Bartholomew Fair, Ben Jonson,
25, 32
Basse, William, 156, 157
Battle of Agincourt, The, 97
Beaumont, Francis, 68–87, 107
—— and Fletcher, 68–87, 113
——, Sir John, 107, 108
——, Sir John (the younger),
107

Bedford, S. Daniel's *Epistle to the Countess of*, 11
Beggar's Bush, The, Fletcher and Massinger, 82
Bloody Brother, The, Fletcher, 78, 79
Bond, Mr. Warwick, 156
Bondman, The, 206
Bonduca, Fletcher, 78, 79
Bosworth Field, Sir J. Beaumont, 107, 108
Brathwait, Richard, 109-112
——, Sir Strafford, 109
Breton, Nicholas, 15-17
Brewer, Anthony, 133-137
Bridges, Mr. Robert, 62
Britain's Ida, 149-151
Britannia's Pastorals, W. Browne, 151-155
Brooke, Lord. *See* Greville
——, Christopher, 157, 182, 185
Browne, William, 151-157, 182, 185
Bullen, Mr. A. H., 17, 89, 90, 127, 128, 174
Bussy d'Ambois, G. Chapman, 40, 41

C

Camden, William, 24
Campion, Thomas, 35, 89-93
Carew, Richard, 8
——, Thomas, 27
Catiline's Conspiracy, Jonson, 24, 30-32
Cervantes, proof of early popularity, 76
Challenge for Beauty, Heywood, 119, 127
Changeling, The, Middleton, 126
Chapman, George, 8, 24, 39-46, 133, 165, 173
Chess, A Game at, Middleton, 126, 128

Chettle, Henry, 174
Christ's Victory and Triumph, G. Fletcher, 138-144
Christian turned Turk, A, Daborne, 176
Chronologer, City—his duty, 26, 125, 191
Churchyard, Thomas, 4
City Madam, Massinger, 216
Cockayne, Sir Aston, 83
Cœlica, Lord Brooke, 197, 198
Coleridge, S. T., 13, 27, 65, 86, 216
——, Hartley, 208
Constable, Henry, 5
Cooke, John, 132
Coriolanus, 20
Craig, Alexander, 106
Cromwell, Oliver, 177
Cumberland, S. Daniel's *Epistle to the Countess of*, 11
Cupid's Revenge, Beaumont and Fletcher, 85
Cymbeline, 20
Cypress Grove, The, Drummond, 106

D

Daborne, Robert, 163, 176, 204
Daniel, John, 114
——, Samuel, 9-14, 23, 35, 62
Davenant, William, 196
Davies, Sir John, 8, 9
Davis, John, of Hereford, 112, 185
Day, John, 173-176
Defence of Ryme, Daniel, 10
Dekker, Thomas, 7, 21-23, 125, 165, 173, 205
Devil's an Ass, The, Jonson, 25, 32
—— *Charter, The*, Barnes, 9
—— *Law Case, The*, Webster, 166, 171

Divine Weeks and Works, Sylvester's translation of Du Bartas, 14

Donne, Dr. John, 47-67, 92, 103, 157, 184, 193; birth and education, 49; marriage and advancement, 50; his effect on versification, 48, 61-64, 67; religion, 58, 59; style, 65

Drayton, Michael, 93-101, 152, 153, 183; place in literature, 93, 94; birth, 94; ill results from *Gratulatory Poem to King James*, 94; Odes, etc., 95-97; characteristics, 100; death, his epitaph, 101

Drummond of Hawthornden, William, 25, 54, 62, 71, 98, 101-106, 174; birth and education, 102; French influence, *ib.*; his verse, 104; sonnet to the Nightingale, *ib.*; Ode of the Ascension, 105; and Jonson, 106

Dryden, John, 30, 32, 37, 54, 67, 79, 106, 178, 185.

Du Bartas, 14, 15

Duchess of Malfy, The, Webster, 160, 166-170

Duke of Milan, The, Massinger, 205, 209-213

Dyer, Sir Edward, 5, 195, 196

E

Eastward Hoe! 24, 40, 165

Elegies of Donne, 55-58

Eliza, Canto on the Death of, G. Fletcher, 137

Elizabethan Poetry, 2, 4, 22

Emblems, Quarles, 191

England's Helicon, 6

English Traveller, The, Heywood, 118-120, 122

Epicene, or the Silent Woman, B. Jonson, 24, 30

Epistles, Daniel, 10-12

——, Donne, 53-55

Epithalamia of Donne, 55

Eugenia, Chapman, 42, 43

F

Faery Queen, The, 139

Fair Maid of the Exchange, The, 134-136

Fair Maid of the West, The, Heywood, 119

Fair Quarrel, A, Rowley and Middleton, 130

Fairfax, Edward, 8

Faithful Shepherdess, The, J. Fletcher, 71, 72

False One, The, Fletcher and Massinger, 80

Fatal Dowry, The, Field, 87, 88, 205

Feast for Worms, A, Quarles, 189, 190

Fidelia, G. Wither, 185, 186

Field, Nathaniel, 87, 88, 176, 204

Fleay, Mr., 27, 73, 81, 124, 133, 174, 175

Fletcher family, 137, 138

——, Giles, the younger, 137-144, 150; birth, 137; career, 138; his religious poems, 137-144

——, John, 68-87, 130, 137, 204, 208; birth and education, 69; first associated with Beaumont, 69; collaboration with Beaumont, 73; later work, 73, 77, 78; associated with Massinger, 79, 81, 82; unaided plays, 81; death and burial, 83; and Daborne, 176

——, Joseph, 151

Fletcher, Phineas, 137, 144-150; relation of his style to Spenser, 149

Florence, The Great Duke of, 206, 215, 216

Flowers of Sion, Drummond, 104-106

Ford, John, 160, 162, 166, 202

Forest, The, Jonson, 25, 37

Freeman, Thomas, 113

Fuller, Thomas, 83, 192

Funeral Elegies, Donne, 56, 57

G

Garden, Alexander, 106

Gardiner, Mr. S. R., 213

Gildon, Charles, 164

Gipsy, The Spanish, Middleton, 126, 127

Goffe, Thomas, 179

Gorges, Sir Arthur, 8, 157, 158

Gough, Robert, 133

Greene's Tu Quoque, 132

Greville, Fulke, Lord Brooke, 194-200; birth and education, 195; success at Court, 196; tragic death, *ib.*; publication of his works, 197; style, 197-200

H

Hadassa, Quarles, 190, 192

Hall, Arthur, 8

——, Bishop Joseph, 9

Hamlet, 18, 19

Harington, Francis, 7

——, Sir John, 7

Harmony of the Church, Drayton, 183

Hazlitt, William, 85, 123

Hector of Germany, The, Wm. Smith, 133

Heir, The, May, 180

Herbert, George, 49

Heywood, Thomas, 116-123; place in literature, 117; birth and education, 118; dramatic works, 118-121; poems, 121-123

Hiren, Barkstead, 112

Hog hath Lost his Pearl, R. Tailor, 176, 177

Holiday, Dr. Barton, 179

Holy Sonnets, J. Donne, 58, 59

Homer, Chapman's translation, 43-46

Honest Man's Fortune, 176

Humour out of Breath, Day, 174

Hunter, Joseph, 93

Huntingdon, Donne's *Letter to the Countess of,* 54

Hymenaei, B. Jonson, 35

Hymen's Triumph, Daniel, 13

Hymns of Astræa, Sir J. Davies, 9

I

I would and yet I would not, N. Breton, 15, 16

Iliads of Homer, G. Chapman, 43-46

Inner Temple Masque, W. Browne, 152, 155

Isle of Gulls, Day, 174

J

Jessopp, Augustus, Dr., 64

Jones, Inigo, 26, 27

Jones, Robert, 114

Jonson, Ben, 23-39, 40, 44, 54, 62, 65, 70, 71, 87, 92, 101, 106, 124, 125, 152, 156, 165, 170, 171, 173, 174, 178, imprisoned, 24; religion, 24;

travels for Sir W. Raleigh,
24 ; Poet-laureate, 25 ; visit
to Drummond, 25, 26 ; City
Chronologer, 26 ; superseded
at Court, 27 ; his death, *ib.*
masterpieces, 27–30 ; Roman
tragedies, 30–32 ; examples
of blank verse, 33–36 ; character of his writings, 38,
39
Julius Cæsar, Shakespeare, 171
——, Alexander, 200

K

Keats, John, on Chapman's
Homer, 44
Ker, Robert, Earl of Ancrum,
106
King and No King, A, Beau-
mont and Fletcher, 73, 76
King Lear, 19
*Knight of the Burning Pestle,
The*, Beaumont and Fletcher,
73, 76

L

Lamb, Charles, 29, 39, 116, 119,
121, 123, 126, 128, 130, 168,
170, 175, 176, 195, 199, 208,
216
Law Tricks, Day, 174
Leighton, Sir William, 114
Lingua, Tomkis, 117
—— and Oliver Cromwell, *ib.*
Locustes, P. Fletcher, 145
Lodge, Thomas, 7, 51
Love's Exchange, Donne, 64
Lucan, Gorges' translation,
158
Lucrece, The Rape of, Heywood,
121
Lyly, John, 5, 7

M

Macbeth, 20
Magnetic Lady, The, Jonson,
27, 33
Maid of Honour, The, Mas-
singer, 205
Maid of the Mill, The, Fletcher,
130
Maid's Tragedy, The, Beaumont
and Fletcher, 73, 74
Malcontent, The, Marston, 165
Man in the Moon, Drayton, 95
Markham, Gervaise, 132
Marlowe, Christopher, 43
*Marriage, Miseries of Enforced,
The*, Wilkins, 132
Marston, John, 22, 40, 113, 162,
184
Mason, John, 113
Masque of Queens, The, Jonson,
35
Masques, The Jacobean, 13, 23,
26, 34–36, 89, 92, 152, 155,
173
Massinger, Philip, 22, 79, 80,
81, 82, 83, 87, 124, 176, 202–
217 ; birth, patronage, 203 ;
education, 204 ; burnt plays,
205, 217 ; publications, 205,
206 ; death and burial, 208 ;
his characteristics, 207, 208 ;
effect on later writers, 216
May Day, Chapman, 41
May, Thomas, 179, 180
Meres, Francis, 98
Mermaid Tavern, 24, 70
Metamorphosis of Tobacco, The,
107
Middleton, Richard, 113
Middleton, Thomas, 21, 26,
123–131, 167 ; birth, early
work, 124 ; city chronologer,
125 ; imprisonment for satire,
126 ; death, *ib.*, character of
his writings, 126

Mildreiados, Quarles, 193
Milton, John, 15, 62, 138, 142,
    143, 145, 155
Mirrha, Barkstead, 112
Mirror for Magistrates, 94, 113
Monsieur d'Olive, Chapman, 40,
    41
Monsieur Thomas, Fletcher, 81
Moses in a Map of his Miracles,
    Drayton, 94
Muffet, T., 124
Musæus, 44
Muses' Garden of Delights, The,
    Jones', 114
Mustapha, Lord Brooke, 197,
    200

N

Nero, 178, 179
New Inn, The, Ben Jonson,
    26, 33
New Way to pay Old Debts, A,
    Massinger, 205, 209, 213-215
Niccols, Richard, 113
*Nimphidia, or the Court of
    Fairy*, 97
Nobody and Somebody, 133
Nosce Teipsum, Davies, 9, 112

O

Odyssey, Chapman, 44, 45
Old Fortunatus, Dekker, 21
Orchestra, Sir J. Davies, 8
Othello, 19, 20
Overbury, Sir Thomas, 115
Owl, The, Drayton, 94, 95

P

Panegyric, S. Daniel, 10, 11
Parliament of Bees, The, Day,
    173, 175, 176

Parliament of Love, The, Mas-
    singer, 206
Peele, George, 113
Pembroke, Epitaph on Countess
    of, 156
Pericles, Shakespeare, 21, 132
*Philarete, Fair Virtue, The
    Mistress of*, Webster, 184, 186
Philaster, Beaumont and Flet-
    cher, 73, 75, 76
Phillips, 198
Phœnix, The, Middleton, 124
Piscatory Eclogues, P. Fletcher,
    145
Poems, Drummond, 103
Poetry, Campion's *Observations
    in the Art of English*, 92
Poetical Essays of S. Daniel, 10
Poly-Olbion, M. Drayton, 97,
    98-100, 153
Pope, Alexander, 52, 67, 181
Progress of the Soul, The, Donne,
    52
Pseudo-Martyr, Donne, 49
Purple Island, The, P. Fletcher,
    138, 145, 146-149

Q

Quarles, Francis, 188-194 ; as a
    verse-writer, 188, 189 ; birth,
    convictions, marriage, 189 ;
    Biblical paraphrases, 190,192 ;
    employments, death, 191 ;
    elegies, 192-194
Queen's Arcadia, The, S. Daniel,
    12, 13

R

Raleigh, Sir Walter, 8, 24, 158
Ram Alley, Barry, 132
Renegado, The, Massinger, 206,
    207

Revenger's Tragedy, The, C. Tourneur, 159, 161, 162, 164
Roman Actor, The, Massinger, 206
Ronsard, Pierre de, 102
Rowlands, Samuel, 17, 18, 112
Rowley, Samuel, 132
Rowley, William, 119, 124, 125, 126, 128, 129–131, 174
Rule a Wife and Have a Wife, Fletcher, 82
Ryme, Defence of, S. Daniel, 10

S

Sackville, Lord Buckhurst, 8
Saintsbury, Mr. George, 12, 112, 150
Sannazaro, 149
Satires of J. Donne, 49, 51, 52
Satyr, The, B. Jonson, 23
Scott, Sir Walter, on Jonson, 37
Scottish poetry, 101
Scourge of Venus, The, 112
Second Maiden's Tragedy, The, 133
Sejanus, his Fall, B. Jonson, 23, 24, 31, 33, 171
Selden, John, 24, 98, 152
Shakespeare, 18–21, 23, 38, 73, 84, 85, 113, 114, 117, 125, 130, 132, 133, 156, 171, 173
Sharpham, Edward, 132
Shepherd, N. Breton's, *The Passionate*, 15, 16
Shepherd's Hunting, The, Wither, 185, 186
Shepherd, Jonson's, *The Sad*, 36
Shepherd's Pipe, The, W. Browne, 152, 155, 157
Shirley, James, 41, 203
Sicelides, P. Fletcher, 145
Sidney, Sir Philip, 195, 196, 203
Sir Giles Goosecap, 134

Smith, Wentworth, 133
——, William, 133
Sonnets, Shakespeare's, 21
Southwell, Robert, 6
Spenser, Edmund, 139, 149, 152, 154, 158
Staple of News, The, Jonson, 26, 32
Stephen, Mr. Leslie, 202
Still, John, 4
Stirling, Earl of. *See* Alexander.
Suckling, Sir John, 38
Swetnam, Joseph, 134
Swetnam the Woman-hater, 134
Swinburne, Mr. A. C., 21, 27, 30, 32, 39, 43, 132, 133, 167, 168
Sylvester, Joshua, 14, 15

T

Tailor, Robert, 177
Tale of a Tub, Ben Jonson, 27, 33
Tears on the Death of Moeliades, Drummond, 103
Tears of Peace, The, Chapman, 42
Technogamia; or, The Marriage of the Arts, Holiday, 179
Tempest, The, Shakespeare, 20
Tethys's Festival, S. Daniel, 13
Thierry and Theodoret, Fletcher, 81
Tieck, 133
Timon of Athens, 20
Tomkins. *See* Tomkis.
Tomkis, John, 177, 178
Tourneur, Cyril, 133, 159–164, 176; characteristics, 159–160; lost works, 162–163
Townsend, Aurelian, 27
Transformed Metamorphosis, The, Tourneur, 162
Translations of Chapman, 39, 43–46

Travels of Three English Brothers, Day, 174

Troilus and Cressida, Shakespeare, 20

Turk, The, Mason, 133

Two Noble Kinsmen, The, Beaumont and Fletcher, 73, 76

Twyne, Thomas, 7

U

Ulysses and the Siren, Daniel, 12

Underwoods, Ben Jonson, 37

Unnatural Combat, The, Massinger, 206

V

Valentinian, Fletcher, 78, 79

Valour, N. Breton's, *The Honour of*, 15

Venus and Adonis, 150

Virgin Martyr, Massinger, 22, 205

Vision of the Twelve Goddesses, S. Daniel, 12

Volpone or the Fox, Ben Jonson, 24, 27–29, 70

W

Walton, Izaak, 49, 58

Ward, Mrs. Humphrey, 200

Warner, William, 4

Watson, Thomas, 5

Webster, John, 41, 160, 164– 173, 206; birth, 194; collaboration with Dekker, 165; works, 165–166; death, 166; his style, 166–172; period of activity, 172–173

Westward Hoe! Webster and Dekker, 165

Wheeler, Elegy on Sir Edmund, 193

White Devil, The, Webster, 165, 169, 170

Wife, A, Sir T. Overbury, 115

Wild Goose Chase, The, Fletcher, 81

Wilkins, George, 21, 132, 174

Winter's Tale, The, Shakespeare, 20

Witch, The, Middleton, 125, 126

Wither, George, 181–188; place in poetry, 181; birth and education, 182; imprisoned for *Abuses Stript and Whipt*, 183, 184; lack of self-criticism, 187, 188

Woman, A Very, Massinger, 81

Woman is a Weathercock, Field, 87, 88

Woman-hater, The, Beaumont, 70, 71

Woman Killed with Kindness, Heywood, 118, 120

Women Beware Women, Middleton, 125, 127–129

Women Pleased, Fletcher and Massinger, 80

Wood, Anthony à, 113, 182, 204

Woodhouse, Peter, 113

Wyatt, Sir Thomas, Webster and Dekker, 165

LONDON : PRINTED BY WILLIAM CLOWES AND SONS, LIMITED,
STAMFORD STREET AND CHARING CROSS.